7.15

P9-DMB-453

WITHDRAWN

WITHDRAWN

THE

REAPER

AUTOBIOGRAPHY OF ONE OF THE
DEADLIEST SPECIAL OPS SNIPERS

NICHOLAS IRVING
WITH GARY BROZEK

ST. MARTIN'S PRESS 🐾 NEW YORK

This is a true story, though some names and details have been changed.

THE REAPER. Copyright © 2015 by Nicholas Irving. All rights reserved. Printed in the United States of America. For information, address St. Martin's Press, 175 Fifth Avenue, New York, N.Y. 10010.

www.stmartins.com

The Library of Congress Cataloging-in-Publication Data is available upon request.

ISBN 978-1-250-04544-7 (hardcover)
ISBN 978-1-4668-4407-0 (e-book)

St. Martin's Press books may be purchased for educational, business, or promotional use. For information on bulk purchases, please contact the Macmillan Corporate and Premium Sales Department at 1-800-221-7945, extension 5442, or write to specialmarkets@macmillan.com.

10 9 8 7 6 5 4 3

Contents

THE REAPER

Prologue

The sound of my pager cut through the fog of my sleep. I sat up, bone weary and achy, and slipped into my combat precision pants, adjusting the kneepads as I hopped toward my boots and other gear. Grabbing my rigger's belt with one hand and shrugging into my combat shirt with the opposite arm, I felt for the magazine pouches I'd clipped on. As the rest of the members of my Third Ranger Battalion squad made their way down the hallway for the mission brief, I felt the fog lifting. It was go time, and the adrenaline rush cascaded down my legs, making them hum with low-voltage electricity.

I took my usual spot in the ready room, second row to the right of the screens, and adjusted my elbow pads. My spotter, Pemberton, took his place beside me. We nodded at one another and smiled, acknowledging an unstated fact of our current life in Helmand Province. This was shaping up to be as up-tempo as it gets.

"*Groundhog Day,* man. It's like freakin' *Groundhog Day.*"

The old movie that Bill Murray was in about being caught in a time warp. Waking up every day to the same thing over and over again. I was more of a fan of *Stripes,* but I knew what Pemberton was going on about.

Call it the luck of the draw, good timing (or bad timing, depending on your perspective), but three days in, this was definitely shaping up not to be one of those usual deployments where you spend your time going to the gym three times a day, hanging out with the guys, and thinking about all the things you're missing out on back home. We had no time for that kind of overthinking. Even in that first week, we'd gotten into a good rhythm. We'd get back inside the wire just as the rest of the guys were getting up, prep and clean, and then sleep the day away before getting the call for that night's operation.

That early into a three-and-a-half-month deployment, our minds had adjusted but our bodies hadn't. I sat there waiting for the team leader to start the briefing. I rubbed the flat of my palms into my eye sockets, hoping to clear my vision and produce some kind of moisture that would prevent my lids from scraping my eyeballs every time I blinked. Vision, for a sniper especially, was crucial, particularly since we were continually operating at night. Utilizing the cover of darkness did more than help us evade the Taliban; it helped us avoid the punishment the heat and the altitude handed out. Still, the body has its rhythms and cycles, and being active during the night still had us slightly off balance.

Fortunately, the briefing lived up to its name—it was over in a matter of minutes. We went over the terrain—we'd be operating in fairly open and level ground. We also got a capsule summary of the target—a high-value member of the Taliban who was instrumental in supplying a nearby bomb- and improvised explosive device (IED)-making depot. In order to hit this objective, we were going to have to insert on an offset—about five clicks to the north of the village where our intel told us the target was hiding out.

What no one had to tell Pemberton and me was that we were riding a bit of a winning streak. With the exception of one, the rest of the operations had gone off without a hitch, and though we were the only sniper pair among the forty men in the platoon, we were proving our value. The atmosphere in the ready room reminded me of my days in high school playing football back home in Maryland. Even then I was kind of a secret weapon. I was no monster standing over six feet tall and weighing more than two hundred pounds—neither then nor now. I was a little guy, a speedster to an extent, but someone whose primary skills were stealth and the ability to stay cool when the shit hit the fan. This was war, of course, and not a game, but the parallels were there in my mind and in that room. We were meshing as a team. The early-season jitters had been reduced if not entirely eliminated. We wanted to see action, and we'd proved ourselves capable of taking it to the enemy with precision. Confidence is one thing; cockiness is another. No one in that room crossed the line beyond a quiet assurance that we were going to get this done, and we were all going to be back in a half-dozen or so hours, joining the nonsleepers in watching a movie or playing some Xbox games.

I can't say that the same we-got-this-no-need-to-worry-'bout-it attitude existed with the short-timers. When you could count your days left in-country on two hands, when the countdown was real and not just something that floated ahead of you like some fuzzy ghost of an object in your night vision, that's when your thoughts were like those proverbial cats that avoided being herded.

Also, I never expected to become the Third Ranger Battalion's deadliest sniper when that three-and-a-half-month tour of duty ended. All my life I'd dreamed of one day joining the military and fighting to defend my country. That I achieved some notoriety is partly due to luck and timing, but it is mostly due to the fact that I received extraordinarily good training.

In a lot of ways, I was the least likely candidate to become the guy who became known as "the Reaper." I heard a lot of stories about me and my exploits. As is true in lots of branches of the military, myths and legends grow. I had to laugh the time I heard that someone had attributed more than seven hundred kills to me. Not that I wouldn't have wanted to have made that kind of contribution to helping keep my comrades-in-arms safe, but it's important to keep things real. Thirty-three is real.

That's why I wanted to write this book and to share with readers my experiences. The first time I heard myself referred to as the Reaper was after an operation not so different from the one that I just described. I liked the name and took pride in it, but in the late hours after first hearing that name, I thought about some of the things I'd done and experienced that brought me to the point where I'd earned that recognition. As I said, I was in many ways both the least likely and someone who seemed destined to make it as a sniper. I come from a military family, I'd read books and watched films that celebrated the exploits of past military heroes, could name every weapon used in our country's wars, yet I struggled with some physical limitations that nearly saw me not get out of basic training. I also made my share of newbie mistakes—including nearly taking on a U.S. tank that I mistakenly thought was an enemy Iraqi vehicle, and pushing the magazine release instead of the trigger the first time I fired a weapon in anger on the battlefield. I also sometimes struggled with the authoritarian nature of military life and committed a few youthful indiscretions.

As a young person I'd romanticized war and as a young adult I'd witnessed its harsher realities. In the pages to come I share stories that reveal that the Reaper is far more complicated than a name and a number. In doing so, I hope that I can pay tribute to the men I knew who lost their lives and the countless others who made the ultimate sacrifice. As I said, I was fortunate that my time deployed to Iraq and more especially in Afghanistan in 2009 coincided with a period of heightened activity. Success is a matter of opportunity being seized. Though I've been credited with those kills, I know that I wouldn't have a story to tell if it weren't for a whole bunch of other people who made sure that when I was placed in that situation, I could perform. To them and to so many others who came before and whose contributions I have no way of knowing, all I can say is thank you.

1. They Call Me the Reaper

The test we faced that third night working in support of Charlie Company, First Platoon, in Kandahar was not the first one and it wasn't going to be the last. In fact, long before I rose through the army's ranks to become a direct action sniper, I was constantly faced with challenges. To one degree or another, that's probably true of most people in just about any walk of life. Except that for me, so much of it took place in a short period of time. I enlisted right of out of high school in 2004 and then served in various capacities with the Third Ranger Battalion after getting through the Ranger Indoctrination Program (RIP)—machine gunner, machine gun team leader, grenadier, team leader, designated marksman, sniper, sniper team leader, and master sniper.

During the three-and-a-half-month period from May of 2009 through August of that year, when I tallied more than thirty-three kills, I was about three months shy of turning twenty-four years old. On and off, I'd been deployed to Iraq and Afghanistan since 2005; I married in 2007; and I'd gone through more schools and training programs than somebody who'd gone the other route and attended college as an undergraduate and then as a graduate. I like to think that I learned a whole lot, and I'm sure I did, but while it was all going on, I felt like I was a rock rolling downhill, gathering momentum, tearing up a few things around me, and accumulating a few things that stuck to me. Some of it was painful; some of it was fun; and like anybody who'd been rolling along like that, I was feeling a bit dizzy.

As you can imagine, especially during that period that earned me the nickname "the Reaper," I didn't have a whole lot of time to sit back and reflect on everything that had happened to me that put me in that hot zone. I knew that it was the luck of the draw that had us seeing so much action.

A lot of guys at Fort Benning told us when they learned that we were being deployed to Kandahar that we needed to be prepared to be bored out of our minds. I was also fortunate that I was with Charlie Company, First Platoon. After all, that was the unit that I grew up with in battalion. I knew most of the guys I was going to be assigned with. We'd been deployed together before, and they were really, really good guys, squared away. In some ways this was going to be different. I had rank now and I'd be one of the men planning missions, giving briefings. I felt prepared for that, but I also knew that with leadership came responsibility. You don't serve in the armed forces without having a sense of responsibility for your fellow soldiers, but this was going to be at a different level. I wasn't always the most responsible kid and I liked to have a good time still, and I told myself that I wasn't going to change too much.

You're always on edge predeployment. When word came down that we were going to Kandahar, we all met the news with a mixture of relief and curiosity. The Second Ranger Battalion was currently over there, and their guys were reporting back that things were very quiet. A few missions. Not really getting shot at.

I should clarify something. The sense of relief I mentioned. That was mostly what we told our wives and girlfriends. I told my wife, Jessica, that this was going to be a boring deployment, probably my last one. I'd be away just a few months and then we'd figure out the next steps. Afghanistan sucks. You hardly ever see anybody; they all live hidden in the mountains. Kandahar is a city. Don't worry.

In truth, I was pissed for all the reasons stated above. I wanted to get into as much stuff as possible. That's what I'd been spending all these years busting my ass off preparing to do. You become a sniper; you want to shoot. You want to do your job. So, along with the anxiety I was feeling, there was some disappointment and frustration. It didn't help that all around the base we're hearing from some other guys who'd been assigned to Forward Operating Base (FOB) Wilson as well as others in Kandahar that we better take our Xboxes and our PlayStations, and we'd better load every hard drive, zip drive, and any other kind of digital storage device we had with plenty of movies.

A few days later, I was sitting in our old Mercury Grand Marquis inside the brown gate that surrounded the Third Battalion's secret compound at Benning. Jessica was in tears, just a river of them flowing. I felt helpless to really reassure her, and that made me mad at myself. Add that to being frazzled with all that comes with being deployed, all the worry and wonder I had about my new role, and our good-bye was not rom-com worthy. I cried a bit, and felt bad that the two of us had been Stateside together only a few months.

I have to admit that I wasn't always the most pleasant guy to be around when I came back from deployment. Prior to this upcoming deployment, my company and I had been working out of Baghram Air Force Base in support of SEAL Team Six. While at Baghram I'd worked with another Ranger sniper by the name of Pete who really showed me the ropes. He had been in the sniper section for some time and served as the sniper platoon sergeant.

When I'd come back to Georgia, it was like I was in a new world. It always felt like that, but it didn't help that while I was gone, Jessica had rearranged the whole house. I knew that I shouldn't be pissed about that. After all, she was looking for ways to make things better, to help her pass the time waiting, but still. It's hard to flip the switch back to being normal Nick after being downrange. Out in the field, you want to keep everything the same. Keep the routine going.

I knew that I had to flip the switch again. Go back to being that other Nick, the guy who, to be honest, over the five-plus years I'd been in the army, was the easier one to be. So, as I'm standing outside the car hugging Jessica, it is like a scene from a sci-fi movie. She's standing there holding on to me, and a faint, ghostlike image is separating himself from her, already with the other guys on the compound ripping and running around getting all their stuff together, hearing that C-17's engines revving up and idling. Then I really did walk away, giving Jessica one more wave before immersing myself in my other life.

An hour later, I'm settled in. The Ambien-induced sleep had a hold on me, and twenty-three hours later I was in Afghanistan. Bleary-eyed and dry mouthed, I stepped off the transport into a kind of heat that Georgia can't produce—a dry, searing version in which every ounce of moisture has been wrung from the air.

I liked that introduction to this other life. It signaled that the slate was wiped clean. This was not the States. When I looked around as we offloaded and then loaded to make our way to the FOB, nothing seemed at all familiar. Gone was the lush spring landscape of Georgia. No matter where I looked I wasn't going to find a paved road, a white picket fence framing the driveway, and the cluster of mailboxes at our apartment complex, no whine and whirr of insects. Just the heat and the smell, a mixture of hay and manure. This is where the other Nick, the one who'd become the Reaper, could call home. I didn't need reminders of my real home that would get my memory working. I was entering my workplace, and I didn't need any more distractions.

I also liked that Pemberton and I were being housed in an area that was fenced off from the rest of the base. All the troops were in our own kind of walled city, cement Jersey barriers, metal gates, shipping containers, what seemed miles of chain-link fence and concertina wire. If this was going to be a boring deployment, at least we had a nice setup. Pemberton and I found our private rooms in what resembled a simple aluminum two-story apartment building.

"Not too bad," I said to myself when I opened the door. I had a few storage-locker-type closets, a bed, a desk, and chairs in a room that was about twelve by fifteen feet. Even though I was trying not to think about home, I was struck by how much it reminded me of the bedroom I'd had growing up as a kid in Maryland. My dad was an E6 stationed at Fort Meade. We lived in a modest house in Jessup, Maryland, where it was just my dad, my mom, and my sister, Jasmine. My parents had met in Augsburg, Germany, where they were both stationed. My mom was an E4, but I don't remember her in uniform at all. By the time I was old enough to start school, she'd left the military to be a full-time mom. Money was always tight, so Mom worked for UPS and Burger King, among other jobs, to help make ends meet.

Growing up on base and living in military housing didn't seem at all unusual to me. It was what I grew up with and what most of the kids I hung around with as a preschooler knew. Some of my first memories are of being on that base and going to work with my dad sometimes. I didn't know what he did, all I knew was that the American flag went up every morning and we'd salute it. I was taught to show respect to everyone and especially to the men and women in uniform and to that flag flying above our neighborhood. In a way it was like we lived in Major Roger's neighborhood. Those preschool lessons were spoken but mostly unspoken. Only later, when I went to the local elementary school, middle school, and high school, would I realize that the air of respect that permeated the base wasn't the same one that existed off base.

As I stowed my gear at FOB Wilson, it was like I had to pack away some of those memories. Never the neatest kid in the world, I remember having my desk at school end up overflowing with homework papers, books, folders, and assorted junk. Not at home of course. That was the place that I had to keep squared away. Probably my greatest accomplishment in elementary school, besides advancing from grade to grade (barely), was meeting Jessica. I was one of the smaller kids in class, but I towered over her. Even at the age of six, as small as she was, Jessica was as energetic and vibrant as any of the kids in our class. She had an awesome smile that she flashed as she ran around the playground during recess, a tiny dynamo daring anybody to keep up with her.

I'd brought along a picture of the two of us when we were still dating and out for the day at Ocean City. A couple of kites are flying above our heads in the perfect blue sky, but it's Jessica's smile that outdazzles everything. I set the frame on the desk and resumed unpacking. From the twin building next door came the sound of barking, a fierce and insistent demand. In a way, another reminder of home. I'd always liked having dogs around and on previous deployments I'd seen how effective working dogs could be in helping us complete our missions. I also liked how they acted a lot like us. As soon as they had their kit on, you could see a change in their attitude. They were all business. They sat up straighter, their ears peaked to their highest point, their noses twitched, and it was as if their vision narrowed.

I'd been thinking about how businesslike I needed to be in my new role. As much as I'd always wanted to be in the military and had had to grow up very, very fast and learn to do things the right way, I didn't want to come across as too much of a hard-liner. I was going to be in charge, but the key word in that sentence was "I." I still had to be myself, still had to be the guy everyone called "Irv." I'd been exposed to a few different leaders in my time, and I knew what it was like to be led. Nobody wants to feel like they're being ordered and bossed around and that they have no say in how things are going to go down. The reality was that somebody had to be in charge and that the chain of command was a necessary, and often very good, thing. We all had our parts to play, but I was more than a rank and title and so were the guys I was there to help protect. Keep it simple and keep it real was going to be the order of my day.

My thoughts about how I was going to handle this new role were interrupted by the sound of my beeper going off. Leaving the task of organizing my room wasn't something I was comfortable with, but another, and far more important, duty was calling. I grabbed my go kit and weapon and headed over to Pemberton's room. I nudged open the door with my shoulder and then stood there shaking my head. He was standing in front of a small mirror combing his closely cropped gray-streaked dark brown hair.

"Dude, this won't be no photo op. I know you want to look good for the overheads."

The sound of boots clattering down the aluminum stairs was nearly deafening. Ignoring my wise-ass remarks, my spotter said, "So much for boring, right?" He looked at his watch. "Thirty hours ago I was in my rack at home."

We joined the flow of guys into the ready room. Instead of taking my seat with them, I lingered near the front. I scanned the wood-paneled room and the six large-screen displays that had various satellite feeds and other data streaming onto them. Next to me was a large poster-type board, about the size of one panel of school chalkboard. On it were photos of various bad guys. Some of them had a big red *X* through the image. The photos weren't posted haphazardly; they were organized into a type of flow chart with lines connecting some of the images to show relationships among and between the various Taliban enemies we'd been encountering.

I had a couple of topographical maps in my hand and I pushed at the end of the rolled tubes, extending them like a drill bit. I was gathering my thoughts while still eyeing the screens, watching the predator drones while also wondering how it was that the smell of pine could still be so strong. A whole lot of sweaty, smelly men had been in that room, and I thought that maybe the whole paneling thing served as a kind of room freshener. The Special Forces version of those tree-shaped car deodorizers.

I was still new to my leadership role and I also knew what it was like to be one of the guys in the seats. They respected you if you were real, still the same guy they'd known back before you were standing out front. That point was driven home when the platoon leader, whom we were there in support of, kept dropping AFI bombs (another f---ing inconvenience) and a bunch of other acronyms when talking about our ORP (objective rally point). He was a good soldier, but that wasn't how I would handle things, with all the fancy lingo and by-the-book stuff.

I flashed again on that photo of Jessica and me. In it, I was wearing a Dallas Cowboys jersey. I've always loved the 'Boys despite growing up near D.C. and the Redskins. I also loved the game itself and had fond memories of high school days out on the field. In a way I wished these kinds of sessions could be as simple as our pregame chalkboard talks had been. A lot less was at stake back then, of course, and it was easy to just get us hyped up so we'd charge hard and play with more guts than brains. Still, something about that approach appealed to me.

As I scanned the room, preparing my remarks, I remembered what it was like back in the day playing sandlot football. We'd all kneel down and I'd often be the one diagramming plays in the dirt. You do a stop-and-go. You run a post. You stay the hell out of the way.

While my presentation wasn't that informal, I had the guys laughing a little bit when I opened with, "Dudes, listen up," to help set the right tone. I sprinkled in a bit of army lingo—sectors of security, cover and concealment, lines of advance—just to show the guys who didn't know me that I knew my stuff. I told them that our high value target (HVT) was a suicide-vest maker. That got their attention, and I told them the obvious but necessary thing. "Likely, he'll be wearing one or have one close by." That fact seemed to get everybody's attention, and it was good to have them all amped up.

The plan was relatively simple. We knew the HVT's

location. We'd all advance together, and then, about three hundred to five hundred meters from the objective, we were going to break off the sniper element. The assault force would proceed, but the snipers were going to climb onto the top of the building. From there we'd have a better perspective on the entire objective. I concluded my remarks the way I would have if I was talking to the guys back inside the wire. "Okay, we knock that out and pop on the helicopters."

I made eye contact with a few of the guys I didn't know already. Kopp. Fredericks. Gilliam. Howard. They all met my gaze and nodded.

"Good to go then."

Whatever anxiety I was feeling was gone. The briefing went well, and now it was on to the fun part. That began with climbing into the Chinook helicopter for insertion. I'd never flown one of the newer MH47-G variants. They were a step up even from the CH47-Fs. Both were used widely with Special Forces operations, but with the addition of the FLIR (forward looking infrared) and multimode radar, the MHs were ideal for nighttime, low-light, and foul-weather operations. We were definitely going to encounter the first two of those, and who knew about the third?

Given my interest in all things military, particularly weapons and machinery, I'd sat and talked with lots of pilots over the years. I'd been told previously that the CH47s, no matter the variant, were a better fit than the Black Hawks. They were more powerful for one thing, and without a tail rotor, they were less susceptible to the crazy winds in Afghanistan. Most important was that they had a safety feature that also worked well with the weather and terrain in Afghanistan. Windstorms could whip up the sand and soil and brown-out conditions were fairly common. The CH47s had a system that would enable the pilots to switch over to an automatic landing mode that they could use in those low-visibility conditions. It was nice to know that no matter what, we'd be in good hands—human or electronic.

I could feel the adrenaline buzz begin as soon as I approached the aircraft. That special sense of sharpness had begun when I'd gotten my kit on. I'd checked my batteries, my plates, and my night vision, doing my own version of preflight inspection. Now, walking up the ramp at the back of the helicopter, those twin Honeywell engines blasting in my face like the most intense hair dryer in the world, I took my seat knowing that it was now game time. We'd done our thing in the locker room, but that was that and this was this. My leg started bouncing in anticipation. Those weren't my nerves kicking in. This was going to be fun.

Along with that thought, another one joined the party. Every time I was about to set out on an operation my mind turned back to the guys I knew at home, some of my teammates on the football team, other buddies. I wondered what they were doing just then. I knew that I was doing something totally cool. Something few people ever have the opportunity to do. Not only that, I was a leader now, and I was responsible for the safety of other grown men. How cool was that?

Of course, I also thought of my family. I knew they were all proud of me and how I'd risen through the ranks. My parents had never put pressure on me to join, but my dad had definitely been influential in my interest in warfare and weaponry. He fully supported my paperback book habit and let me raid his library. I'd always been interested in the Special Forces and read a lot of Vietnam-era memoirs by guys who were part of the LRRPs, MACV SOGs, SEALs, and Green Berets. I thought that their jungle cammies were so cool and loved how they'd darken their faces to blend into that densely foliaged environment. Living in Maryland, I could kind of sense what it would have been like to live in that hot and humid environment. My previous tours in Iraq and Afghanistan had exposed me to another kind of hostile environment entirely. Now, in the helicopter, I got to experience a bit of what Vietnam might have been like. The smell of the guys, gun oil, and the chopper's hydraulics and engine fluids were all superheated. I also thought I could smell everyone's excitement, and I looked around at their amped-up eyes, wondering if they were thinking what I was thinking.

Not all our talk was about warfare. For the first few minutes of the flight, the chatter was at its usual level. Over the sound of the rotors and the engine, I could hear a few guys talking about their picks. The NFL season had just ended in February 2009, with the Steelers beating the Cardinals, but the diehards were already talking about their fantasy draft picks.

"I'm going to grab my Holmes boy, and that's the end of the discussion."

"Cardinals can't win the big one. You saw what Roethe-lisberger did. Piles up the numbers."

"You don't know jack about anything."

After a while their voices became as much white noise as the helicopter's sounds. I sat there and ran my hands along the stock of my weapon. Pemberton spotted me and smirked. "A little foreplay with Dirty Diana?"

I'd named my SR-25 a while ago and even that early into the deployment, thanks to Pemberton, everyone in the platoon knew it. He also knew that I didn't like his Win Mag at all. I was okay with bolt-action rifles like his, but I preferred the semiautomatic and felt like I shot so much better with my SR.

"Mike," I said, using Pemberton's first name as a way to let him know I wasn't messing around. "Show some respect for my girl. Just because you're stuck with that butt-ugly green Win Mag doesn't mean you have to be all up and jealous. You already turned that thing green with envy, so don't look to drag us down."

I really did hate how Pemberton's weapon looked. It was just a dull green. It had no personality whatsoever. In a way it was kind of like Pemberton. Quiet and no-nonsense, nothing that was going to attract anybody's attention. That was the initial impression Pemberton gave off, but there was a lot more to him than that.

"Dude." Pemberton just shook his head slowly. "You've got some issues."

I wouldn't have called my treatment of my weapon an issue. Jessica might have if I'd told her that the reason why I'd sometimes stay late after work was because I'd applied a new coat of paint to it. I would stay at work for three, four, or five extra hours just painting various colors and patterns on this rifle. I wanted every little piece to look perfect. If there was an edge that was not painted correctly or crooked, I'd start the whole thing over again. I had to have had at least thirty coats of paint on this gun by that point. It was thick. I didn't want it to bang up on something, so that it would go back to its original, all-black color. If it did get chipped a little bit, there would still be a little bit of paint underneath it, so I could easily fix it. I would change the pattern at least once every two weeks.

Pemberton, on the other hand, needed nearly constant reminding that he needed to clean his gun.

I ran my finger along the brown and black tiger stripes that were Dirty Diana's present outfit. I figured I was going to have plenty of time for the gun's care and feeding since this was most likely going to be one of those deployments where I'd be looking for ways to pass the time.

I saw Pemberton take his helmet off and run his fingers through his hair. The first time I saw the guy back in garrison, the thing that struck me was his long hair. It gave him the air of a lady's man, which he was, and a kind of sophistication that a lot of the other guys lacked. Part of that came from him being a prior service guy. He'd been in the navy and toured around the world basically. He hadn't seen any kind of combat, but traveling to all those places, experiencing all different kinds of cultures, made him worldly in ways that neither I nor many of the other guys were.

Pemberton was older than me and, though I outranked him and he was my spotter, we didn't have that kind of strict top-dog pilot/copilot relationship. We were more or less equals, not like the golfer/caddy situation that marks how some sniper teams operate. He would take shots just as much as I did. The unusual thing about battalion snipers and spec ops snipers was the fact that we really don't have the traditional spotter, where he knows everything there is to know about the environment, the gun, the bullet, and everything, and all the sniper has to do is listen to him and then pull the trigger. We had to be a spotter and sniper all in one, big ball. Sometimes, we'd have to split off and each operate on our own. I knew that there'd be times when we'd have an objective and we'd have to hit two buildings at once, or we'd go out in support of two assault teams. Pemberton and I would then split off, and I had to trust that he'd get the job done, and he'd have to trust me as well.

I did trust Mike and he was a good guy. A couple of days before we left for this deployment, he was over at our place. He was talking with Jessica and he said to her, "I've got your man covered. He's going to come back."

Jessica wrinkled her nose and said, "How do I know you're telling me the truth?"

Mike ran his hand over his chin. I could hear his skin rustling through his two-day bristle. "Well, I'm afraid of you, so I'll do anything to keep from having to experience your Latina wrath coming down on my head if I come back without him."

He'd only known Jessica for a relatively brief time, but he'd picked up on the fact that she was fiery as habañero chili. He didn't have to say it, but I knew that he'd literally take a bullet for me. I wouldn't tell him this, but I was really glad when the sniper platoon sergeant, a guy named Pacchini, had paired the two of us up back at Fort Benning. At the time, I didn't know Mike at all, except that he was the hair guy who drove a bright green Mustang, the kind of car only a single guy like him could afford. After that, we spent hundreds and hundreds of hours together and a bond had formed.

Stateside, you're always looking at other guys and evaluating them, trying to figure out how they're going to act overseas. If you're out at a bar and something comes up and a guy jumps up to either watch your back or to hustle you out of there, you know that they're going to be good to go when deployed. Mike was that kind of shirt-off-his-back guy. I also liked that he wasn't afraid to ask questions. A lot of guys don't want to appear stupid or uninformed or whatever, and they'd rather keep quiet and pretend they understand when they don't. I guess that was a part of Mike's maturity. Twenty-seven didn't make him ancient and wise, but it did give him some advantages over the rest of us.

When he'd talked to Jessica, he'd confirmed something that I'd been telling her all along, "The guy is loyal. He's like a German shepherd or a pit bull. He'd do anything for me."

Part of the reason why trust and loyalty built up between us was that I have enormous respect for my elders. Mom and Dad always preached that lesson and spending time in South Carolina with my grandparents and aunts and uncles reinforced that. They knew a hell of a lot more about life than I did. All of my male relatives were hunters and crack shots. They all contributed to teaching me weapon safety and respect for the power that guns had.

Because Pemberton was older than me, I had a hard time with the idea that I outranked him. At one point, early on in our pairing as a team, Pemberton said to me, "Hey, Sergeant, can you remind me again of the recommended lead for fast walkers at eight hundred meters?"

"I can, but only if you don't call me 'Sergeant' anymore. Call me 'Irv,' or call me by my first name. We're going to be together in the crap a lot over there. We're going to be hanging out together. I don't want to have this I-outrank-you kind of attitude. We're going to be friends."

I knew he appreciated that, and that the kind of kidding we did with one another, even when around the other guys, made us both feel more at ease. The closer we got to deployment, the more time we spent together. During training, the sniper/spotter teams worked mostly in isolation from the other five or six other pairings, so when you and your spotter are together that much of the day, you better get along well or you could have some really long and painful days. Snipers and spotters don't have to be best buds, but too much tension can make you a hell of a lot less effective. You develop a relationship where you're like brothers, and you know how that can sometimes go. But in the end, you always have each other's backs.

We were competitive, of course, but early on it became clear why I was the sniper and he was the spotter. I'd always kid him about it, and he didn't really like it, but the man had some issues of his own. Three hundred of them to be precise. For some reason, when we were training and out on the range, Pemberton could not hit a target that was three hundred meters away. He could nail something at a grand (one thousand meters) and every other distance with some accuracy, but the three hundred seemed to throw him off big-time. I can't really blame his choice of weapon; after all, other guys used the Win Mag very, very effectively at that distance and others. To its credit, the Win Mag does shoot really tight groups, but for me, it was just too slow. I felt it was a nuisance to have to manually load it and run the bolt back and forth. I figured that there were going to be a lot of times when we'd have to go after multiple targets. Manually racking that bolt every time was going to give the bad guys enough time to go to ground. I wanted to be able to neutralize targets before they knew what hit them.

Even if it wasn't for that issue he had, he knew that I was going to be the primary shooter. We both knew that, regardless of rank, I was the more accurate shot. He had his relationship with his weapon and I had mine. That might sound strange to someone who's never been a sniper or a serious hunter or target marksman, but our guns are so important to us. I wasn't the only one who had named his gun, but I might have been a little more over the top about care and maintenance of my weapon than most. I was very protective of her, and I didn't like anybody messing around with it behind my back. To make sure they hadn't, and I did this as we were flying to our insertion point, I inspected her again. I made sure that the scope ring was exactly as I left it. I also checked the stock to see if the spot of gun grease I'd put there was still intact. If it wasn't I knew somebody'd touched it. I hated people touching her.

A lot like baseball players with their bats, a sniper and his weapon have a way of communicating. You develop a kind of ritual in the way that you handle it and treat it. You take care of it and it will take care of you. Of course, war is no game, and the consequences are more often than not deadly.

The last few minutes to the insertion point, I tried to just empty my mind. I was successful in eliminating any thoughts of home. When I felt us make contact with the ground and we wobbled a bit, it was like someone had given me smelling salts. I was very clear-minded and felt none of the fatigue that I expected I might. Our walk up to the objective was uneventful. When we got to the point where we split off so the assault team could do their thing, I was feeling hesitant. Part of that was due to the fact that even though I'd seen the topographical maps and the satellite images, everything looked slightly different from what I'd pictured. Night vision contributed to that a bit, but having boots on the ground and an eye-level perspective was very different from the intel we used. I wasn't able to identify any of the features that I thought might distinguish one area from another, one building from another. To be honest, at the break-off point, I had no real idea at all where I was and where I was supposed to position myself.

I hope I don't screw this up, I thought. Then I checked myself and told myself to take a deep breath and play it cool.

That seemed to help. I found the building Pemberton and I were supposed to utilize as a point from which we could cover the assaulters. Over the comms, I could hear the team members chatter and then the sound of explosives and the rattle of a metal gate.

I looked at Pemberton, my eyes wide to indicate my surprise.

"That was fast."

We hadn't even gotten our ladder secure.

A moment later, we heard that the target was secured. They'd snatched him up with no problem and were in the process of walking him out. Better to take them that way and get some intel off them than to neutralize them.

We got word from the platoon leader that we were still needed. We were so far ahead of schedule at that point that they were going to radio the helicopters to extract us. The ETA was about fifteen minutes. Pemberton took the ladder off his pack, and a few moments later, we were positioned on the flat roof of one of the houses. The building didn't have a solid roof, just a few boards and slim tree trunks balanced between the exterior walls in a loose weave. The sun was starting to come up, and that had me on edge. Darkness was our friend and when it turned its back on us, that meant bad things could more easily come our way.

Something caught my eye, a slight stirring, and beneath me, I saw movement. A pile of blankets was on the floor and under that, a family had been sleeping. I could see the whites of a couple of pairs of eyes blinking. It was like they were trying to send me some kind of semaphore message. I wondered for a second if maybe Pemberton knew how to interpret that stuff, but I sure didn't. And I was pretty damn sure the Afghanis below me didn't either. I used another form of message to make myself heard loud and clear. I shook my head very slowly and then put one finger to my lips. I also patted the barrel of my gun, but I don't think they needed that reminder.

Ignoring the fact that one of the people below me could have been armed—well, not exactly ignoring that fact so much as hoping they weren't—I resumed my scanning. To my right at about three o'clock, I could see a small stand of stunted and bare trees. Against that dark backdrop, three human figures in white stood out like spotlighted prisoners against a wall. I looked over to Pemberton, and once I caught his attention, I nodded in the direction I'd spotted the three figures. I could see Pemberton barely dip the front of his helmet in acknowledgment.

I looked back and the three figures were close to the ground and then crawling. No one with nothing to hide would be crawling. Still, I had to keep the rules of engagement in mind. A moment later, I got what I was looking for. The lead guy swung around, and in front of him was the barrel of his weapon. Even in that dim light, I could recognize the shape of an AK-47. My first reaction was, Are you kidding me? This is Afghanistan. Things are supposed to be slow and boring out here. I kept squinting, trying to make my vision clearer. The man's movements were so slow and deliberate that the slow-motion effect of it all, my newness to the field of operations, my sleep-deprived but high-adrenaline state had me wondering if I was really seeing what I thought I was seeing.

I took my weapon off safe and called in the sighting.

As I took the slack out of my trigger, I was thinking, *Oh my gosh. This is really about to happen right now.*

I tried to get some moisture worked up in my mouth but I was as a dry as the terrain. Consciously willing myself to breathe steady, I lined my sights square on the lead guy's chest. I had already dialed in my scope to three hundred meters, but this target was maybe fifty to a hundred meters outside that range.

I squeezed the trigger and experienced again that slow-motion effect. The recoil came back and sank deep into my shoulder. The smell of the gas burning out of the suppressor mixed with the sweet smell of the gun oil I use. My eye still focused on the crosshairs in the center of the scope, I watched as the man collapsed, almost as if he was a balloon being popped. At the sound of my fire, the rest of the guys opened up on that tree line. The two remaining fighters started to return fire.

I don't know why, but I took out my ear protection. Everything had seemed too surreal to me up to the point when the sounds of all those rounds being fired made everything seem all too real. Next, my whole body shook as Pemberton fired that Win Mag of his. I followed the path of his bullet and watched as that .300 round removed the head of the second bad guy. I felt in complete control and lined up on the third guy, who was now running away, and fired. The force of the strike sent him sprawling forward and his weapon flew out ahead of him, pinwheeling toward the sunrise. With that, the rest of the guys stopped firing.

All of the shooting took place in about thirty seconds. I didn't have much time to consider everything that had just taken place, but I was struck by how fast it had all gone down. How could a simple capture turn into that? One second I was trying to figure out where the heck I was and the next I'm sighting on guys who had no clue in the world that I was watching them. They were probably figuring they were well concealed and they'd have our guys in their sights in just a minute, and anticipating how surprised we were going to be. We'd turned the tables on them pretty quick.

I still had work to do.

"Mike, face my six. We need a 360 to a mile out."

Out of the corner of my eye, I saw the rest of the guys hustling to get into a defensive perimeter. We were all eager for those Chinooks to come in so we could get the hell out of there. I could hear the thump of the rotors and, in a couple of minutes, saw the helicopters. I kept rolling my shoulders back to get the tension out of them, still scan-

ning with my eyes. Once we got the word to go, Pemberton and I jumped off the building. We didn't want to waste
time scrambling down the ladder. We collapsed the device
and I snapped it onto his back. Not wanting to slow ourselves by looking around, we raced to the Chinook, and my
eyes were on the door gunners with their miniguns and
their 240s, hoping that I wouldn't see them go into action.

Once we were inside, we were airborne in an instant. I
knew that there'd be a time for a debrief and our after action reports (AAR), but for just a minute, I wanted to not
think at all. I was glad to simply feel the vibration of those
motors lifting us up and out of there, out of harm's way.
There would be a time for an accounting later on, but all I
wanted to do then was feel the gratitude for having gotten
out of there safe and sound. Despite my wanting to not
think at all, a pair of thoughts got in under the wire. We'd
done well on our first time out with me as a sniper team
leader. At the time, I was thinking it was pretty likely that
we'd seen the only real live action we were going to see.

2. A Near and Colorful Miss

One of the most difficult parts of going out on night operations was getting some shuteye once we were back inside the wire. Another was connecting to any kind of reality other than what was going on with that small group of guys in that small corner of a larger war. After that first night, I experienced a phenomenon like what I'd experienced a few times as a kid—sneaking into a movie late and trying to figure out what was going on after missing the first few minutes of it. That weird combination of sleeplessness, exhaustion, and dislocation was going to take more than a few days to overcome.

In a way, I liked the whole sink-or-swim/get-tossed-into-the-deep-end-of-the-pool thing that was happening to us. Getting into the action immediately was an effective way of jolting us into recognizing that we really were at war. None of us thought that kind of action was going to continue, but it was what we all hoped we'd be doing, so we wanted to savor those few moments. Once back inside the compound, we all worked on our after action reports. I never liked doing them, but I knew they were necessary, mostly when things didn't go quite as planned. Since that first op had gone so well, I struggled through the paperwork, especially since I was now a team leader and I had to have all my shit more squared away than ever before.

Down the hall from where I sat working alone at my desk, I could hear the raucous sounds of the rest of the guys hooting and hollering, a bunch of "Got some!" and a lot less polite language. I knew that the guys were sitting in the briefing room in front of the wall of screens watching the operation on the monitors. It was like a football team, fresh off a victory, going into the locker room or players' lounge to catch the highlights—the big hits, the touchdowns. During the operation, I wasn't conscious of the fact that nearly everything we did was going to be captured, digitally or otherwise, and subject to review. We knew that the satellites and the drones were there, of course, and utilized the technology to help us out, but it wasn't like having one of the guys help you out or calling in a drop or having the arty take out a target for you.

I didn't really think of it this way at the time, but it was kind of like having your conscience—a carbon fiber, metal, and plastic one—as a kind of running commentary going through your head. You could choose to pay attention to it or not when the operation was going on. Later, like having to do those AARs, it was almost required that you pay attention to what those camera eyes had seen. I think we would have done that kind of review anyway, but having it be up there on the screen kind of distanced you from it. It wasn't like the images ran through your mind as you lay in bed, though that would happen too, they were up there on a screen. Even though you could see yourself in the replays, it was like watching someone else, a character, an icon, a substitute for you that was running through that compound and scaling that wall.

We were, almost to a man, video game guys, so it felt natural to us to see that kind of violent action rendered on a screen. As time went on, I had less interest in watching those videos, but I still did it. We had the regulation AARs to do, then Pemberton and I had our own version of them to do. As the amount of violence we saw and participated in increased, the more important those unofficial reviews became. At least for me they did. I'd done the killing. While I watched them on screen, it was that guy, the one in the video, and not me who was now responsible for those deaths.

Those thoughts would come much later in that deployment. The first morning back was all celebratory, a lot of fist bumps and genuine bravado. We were warriors and we were proud of how we'd done our jobs. Let those images burn into our brains. We didn't need a screen saver to keep that from happening.

But as I sat there with the guys watching the ghostly

black-and-white images on the video, I wondered if they were seeing what I was seeing. More specifically, I was wondering if they were seeing things the way I was seeing them.

It's funny that my ability to see things played a big part in my life—and by "see things" I don't mean seeing dead people or something supernatural. In my case, I'm talking about my vision and what I literally couldn't see that other people could.

I had a bad case of childhood *Navy SEALs*-itis. I saw Charlie Sheen in that movie and it was over for me. That was what I wanted to do with my life. The SEAL teams seemed to have it all—weapons, explosives, cool submersibles, and all the rest. I wasn't into the water part of being a SEAL that much, but I knew that if I disciplined myself and got the necessary training, I could handle it.

You have to understand that "discipline" isn't something that came easily for me. When you're a kid, school dominates your life. I knew that I needed to buckle down and do well in school, but I didn't like school. It was boring. So, although I knew I needed to do well in school, to please my parents mostly and to stay out of trouble, I never really put in the necessary time and effort. I earned one A grade in my entire school career through high school graduation. That was in the Reserve Officers' Training Corps (ROTC) class I took in ninth grade. I think you get the picture of what kind of kid I was.

Prior to seeing that Charlie Sheen SEAL movie, I knew that I wanted to be a sniper. Not many kids make their own ghillie suit in middle school, but I did. I used to scare the crap out of the rest of the kids in the neighborhood when I'd pop up out of nowhere. I had an air rifle with a scope on it, and I terrorized the neighborhood birds with that until my father took it away. That didn't really stop me, and I'd sneak into my parents' bedroom where I knew it was hidden and take it out and use it. It would have been smart of me to restrict my use of that weapon to the outdoors, but I'd fire it in the house, putting little pockmark holes in the wall. I was smart enough to use my sister's Play-Doh to fill in the holes like it was spackle. Good thing the walls in the house were mostly white and my sister was good about not mixing her Play-Doh colors together. I never got caught for that little bit of destruction.

My dad didn't push me into a career in the military. He answered whatever questions I had about it, but I think he saw my interest as a phase that I was going through, one that I'd inevitably outgrow. He did support me in my interest though. Once I made the transition from sniper to SEAL, he'd drive me the couple of hours it took to get to Ocean City, Maryland, so that I could do my open-water swimming training and beach runs. After my senior year in high school, I attended the Navy SEAL Cadet Corps camp down in Florida. I went through and passed the mock Basic Underwater Demolition/Seal (BUD/S) class and took the

Navy SEAL physical fitness test. After I returned home, I went to a navy recruiter and told him to sign me up. I was going to become a Navy SEAL.

A couple of weeks later, I shipped out to Florida, thinking that I was going to join the navy and start down that path. Well, that trip only lasted as long as it took to do a vision test. I aced the visual acuity test and was told that my vision was twenty-twenty. I remember sitting there, after passing the physical and that first part of the vision test, thinking about that SEAL obstacle course, when a navy doctor held up a comb-bound book and asked me what I saw on that first page.

I said, "The number twelve."

She tried to keep her expression neutral, but I could tell that something was up. She flipped to the next page.

"What do you see now?"

I shrugged. "Nothing. Just a blank page."

She went on to explain that I was red-green color-blind. That meant I couldn't be a SEAL. As I thought about it I realized it meant that I couldn't have a career in any branch of the military. I sat there stunned. The only odd thing I could recall was my sister once asking me why I wanted to wear a pair of purple socks to school. I didn't have any purple socks. They were black. Why was she messing with me?

I didn't have too long to sit there feeling sorry for myself. At the recruiting station where the preliminary screening was taking place, other branches of the military were also testing candidates. An army nurse swooped in and led me to her side of the room. You want to be in the army, son? Yes, I do. Then follow me. She used her finger to trace the number on what I thought was a blank sheet of paper, basically helping me cheat my way out of the world of color blindness and into the military. Later, after I got home an army sergeant showed up at the house and gave me the pitch on what the Rangers were, basically SEALs without water. Despite having done all that swimming work, I was okay with that. I just wanted to do cool stuff overseas.

This was post 9-11 and qualified candidates were in short supply, and that army nurse figured, why reject an otherwise well-qualified and highly motivated candidate?

I guess I'm glad that I don't remember that woman's name because she might get in some kind of trouble for helping me into the army that way. Things worked out well, and the issue of my being color-blind never played a part in my career. Good thing the army has limited dress options, otherwise I might have been found out at some point. Either that or I would have had to have my little sister Jasmine enlist with me to serve as my clothes chooser.

Before I went to sleep that night in the hotel room the military provided outside of Fort Meade, Maryland, I was grateful that things had turned out as they had. I'm not saying that I wouldn't have been a valuable SEAL team member and served honorably with them. I was just happy to be a Ranger. Although I let my thoughts wander, I knew that it wasn't a good idea to speculate too much.

After the debrief and going through all the intel and materials we'd collected from the HVT and his locale, Pemberton and I went to breakfast. The chow hall was filled with line guys; most of them had finished and were sitting talking. For Pemberton and me, it was like walking into the school cafeteria as outcasts, kids on the fringe.

We ordered and Pemberton shook his head. "Six eggs? That's not an omelet, that's a henhouse. Where's a little guy like you put it all?"

This was an ongoing topic. I had an appetite out of proportion to my frame.

"I may not be able to eat at all. The smell."

We had three choices of places to eat spread out within the larger compound. The smells coming from the French, Asian, and American spots were mixing in a way that reminded me of the streets of Ramallah, back in the day, during my first deployment.

"It's just cheese."

"Why's it got to be a baguette and not just bread?"

Our take on international cuisine over, we found a table by ourselves and dug in. Between bites and sips, the two of us talked about the night's operation.

"Didn't expect that," I began.

"Weird."

"It is."

I knew that Mike's kill was his first. Not his first overall, but his first with his rifle, relatively close range. Like me, he'd taken out a guy on a previous deployment with the .50 cal., back when he was a private and first joined the battalion. If watching those satellite feeds gave you a sense of detachment, then being the operator on a .50 cal, with a remote-controlled weapons system (RWS), was really like playing a video game. Regardless of what weapon you used, or what range you were at, there was something about your first experiences in combat.

In 2005, we were doing a Ground Assault Force (GAF) operation, taking the Strykers to a location outside of Ramallah. This was my first deployment, so I was a little more gung ho than the rest of the guys. I was still in that stage of cherry new guy where I was hoping to get into one of the big firefights I'd heard about when guys came back Stateside. It all sounded so cool. Most of the firefights I'd participated in to that point had lasted five to ten minutes tops. While we were in them, it seemed like hours, but later when we reviewed the footage, only a few minutes of real-time action had occurred. Most of that was due to the enormous firepower advantage we had. At that point in Iraq, we weren't doing any kind of nation building or advising. It was pure and simple controlled chaos. I liked that. The objective was clear, the rules of engagement were clear, and we went out there and in a controlled but chaotic manner we destroyed things and people. We'd head out at night and a few hours later we were showering.

What took the most time was arresting, searching, and processing detainees. I had done all kinds of training related to destroying or capturing targets; helping gain intel was something I was having to learn more about while on the ground. I would want to talk to the guys about what we were doing, but I picked up on a vibe and listened to it. To them what we were doing was no big deal. Just another day at the office. Just do your job. Don't bring your work back home with you.

As a cherry new guy, I was busting inside with questions. What was it like to shoot someone up close? Do you even think about it?

One night that first deployment, we set out. I'd been trained as a Stryker driver, and it was pretty thrilling to be in control of a forty-ton, eight-wheeled vehicle capable of seventy miles per hour. At that point, though, I was a gunner, stuck sitting in a little pod where all I had was my joystick, my video display, and my team leader Salazar's feet to look at. If I turned around, I could see the other assaulters behind me in the back end of the vehicle.

By this time everything had become routine. We'd reach the objective, offset about a thousand meters from it, drop the ramp, and I'd stay behind to offer cover fire for the assault team. On this particular operation, everything went as smooth as could be. We went in without incident. No shots were fired. We got the guys while they were sleeping and then loaded them up.

The worst part was always the drive to and from the objective. IEDs were the biggest threat, as well as vehicular-borne devices.

Salazar was up top and he said to me, "Hey, I want you to check this car out to the left. Make sure no one gets inside our formation."

Seemingly out of nowhere, a car came flying past us on our left, traveling about seventy miles an hour. We're on Route Tampa, the sun has just come up, and there's light traffic, just a few other vehicles out there. Something was up or maybe some guy just didn't want to be stuck behind our convoy of six Strykers. We were in the lead one and guys were freaking out over the comms, wondering what the hell this dude was up to, where he came from.

Salazar's voice cut through the chatter. "If this guy turns around and approaches us at that same rate of speed, take him out."

I acknowledged his order, but my mind was racing. "Is this serious? Do I really take this guy out? Is it that easy?"

Truth is, I was hoping that the guy would turn toward us. I wasn't wishing that he'd do any damage to us, but I wanted to see what that .50 cal could do. Another part of me was thinking it would be good if the man just kept speeding down the road and out of sight. It was one of those "angel on my right shoulder and devil on my left" situations. For a while, neither of them was winning the debate and the man in the car wasn't cooperating either. He just stopped the car on the side of the road. I zoomed in on him through the gun's scope and I saw his dead clear eyes sizing us up. We were still moving toward him and he was about a half mile away.

That's when he turned the car around and started coming toward us. I thought, "Oh my gosh, this is really going to happen."

He revved his engine and came toward us, but then stopped right in the middle of the road as if he was going to block us.

Salazar started beating on the roof of the Stryker, yelling, "Shoot! Shoot!"

I hesitated, looking at my view screen at this expressionless man. I took the weapon off safe.

I felt Salazar's boot on my shoulder and heard him saying, "Shoot! Shoot the mother——!"

I opened up with a seven-round burst, watching the bullets climb up the car's hood and then into the windshield, and through the smoke of the shattering glass, I saw something explode inside the car. It wasn't an IED; it was the man inside it. He turned into mist and chunks.

We stopped the vehicle and, just like in any operation, the assaulters approached the car acting as they would if they knew the man was still alive. I knew better, but still they needed to be cautious. When the man didn't respond to any of their orders and it was clear that he wasn't going to be able to, they opened the driver's side door and this pile of stuff dropped to the ground. They made their way to the car's trunk and unloaded some AKs and then one of the guys held up the head of a rocket-propelled grenade (RPG). If we had charged the guy and run him over, that RPG could have gone off and done some damage. We didn't know exactly what the guy's intent was, but it didn't matter, both because of what happened to him, what I'd done to him, and because of how he'd chosen to respond to our presence.

A couple of the assaulters congratulated me, and that felt good, but later on, when my shock wore off, I had this funny coppery taste in my mouth, like I was sucking on a penny. I felt a little queasy, with that stomach-sinking feeling you get when somebody gives you some bad news.

Later that night, the image of that man returned to me. I had a dream where I was in a room with a ceiling fan spinning above me. The blades of the fan were the man's four limbs plus his head and chest. He was staring at me with that same dead-eyed stare, but as the fan spun faster and faster, he started screaming at me openmouthed. Eventually the fan got spinning so fast that his limbs were whipped off and he sprayed the room with blood and guts, covering me as well with this gelatinous goo.

I woke up thinking about what my platoon sergeant had told me prior to our going over to Iraq. We were in a

Humvee, with me in the back and him in the front seat. He turned and said, "You know what, Irv?"

"What's up, Sergeant?"

"After you kill a man, there's no other feeling like it. Mark my words. You won't want to do any hunting again. The excitement of that will be gone. You won't find any joy in it either. Once you kill a man, you can't replace that feeling."

He was right. The combination of emotions and the physical rush that floods through your body after combat is unlike anything I'd experienced before or since.

Sitting in the chow hall, I knew that Pemberton was sorting through some of those same thoughts and feelings as a result of that first close-in kill that night. It helped that I was there, even if we weren't talking about his mental state directly.

Pemberton nodded toward a few of the occupied tables. "They don't get it, do they?"

I shrugged. "I doubt it. From what I've heard most of them haven't been outside the wire at all."

"They think they want to be out there."

He left the last part of that unfinished, but I knew what he meant. "Roll of the dice, I guess."

Depending upon how I felt at any particular moment, when our operational tempo proved to be consistently pedal to the metal, I sometimes thought we were rolling double sixes or snake eyes. A lot of the time, though, it was like we were rolling both.

I did tell Pemberton that I had taken the wrong route into the compound that night and that I wouldn't let that kind of thing happen again.

"Walking past that open area along that wall? That was messed up—anything could have been on the other side."

"At least we cleared it."

I appreciated him saying that, but I knew that I didn't want to do anything like that again.

Eight hours or so later, I sat in bed looking at the display on my pager. I decoded the message and was immediately wide awake. I ran across the hallway and banged on Pemberton's door.

"Hey, man. Get ready. I think we're about to go out."

As I made my way down to the ready room, the scene reminded me of something from a movie about Wall Street or some busy office. Guys were trotting and hustling, all of them with papers or shadow light imagery, weapons and ammunition. From top to bottom everyone was excited. Another army unit had taken casualties the night before, and based on the message, we had an important target that had to be taken out ASAP.

I was still in my PT (physial training) shorts and T-shirt, and I joined the first, second, and third squad leaders, the weapons squad leader, and the platoon sergeant, Casey. They were all huddled in front of a sixty-inch flat-screen TV. When I came up, I looked at the images on the screen. A compound wedged into some thick bush and a few individuals milling around in front of a building that was several stories tall. Somebody paused the video and we focused on one individual. We had our man.

Next, we focused on the environment. We debated whether we could do an offset drop with the helicopters or if they should land on the *X*. Everybody contributed and we could all sense that the clock was running, so there wasn't a whole lot of back-and-forth. Each squad leader knew what his team had to do. Pemberton had come into the room, and I split off from the others. As snipers, we had to put ourselves in the most precarious position a lot of times. Personally, I preferred being on top of a building. It gave me the best field of vision, meaning we had the widest coverage. The disadvantage was that we'd be skylining ourselves— we'd be silhouetted against the nighttime sky, offering the enemy a better view of us.

By then I'd gotten used to viewing two- and three-dimensional images on a screen or a document and calculating rough distances. Pemberton and I went over the distances we estimated between buildings, what our points of vulnerability might be.

Meanwhile Sergeant Casey sat at a computer inputting all the different elements of the operation—directions, the roster, who's going on the helicopters, which squads are bringing what equipment. A few minutes after we were done, the battalion commander came down the stairs and handed us each a disk with all the intel on the mission, including maps and photos of the area of operation (AO).

"This is a TST [time sensitive target], men. You're out in thirty minutes."

That gave us just enough time to coordinate with the pilots and get our kit squared away and do a briefing.

Before the brief, I ran upstairs to the freaks and geeks center. That's what I called the room where our computer operations were located. Though I had done some rough figuring myself, I wanted to confirm how environmental factors were going to play into my initial positioning plan. I was glad I wasn't a member of the freaks and geeks squad. I mean no disrespect by calling those guys by that name. They performed an invaluable service, one that I wouldn't have been able to do. If this FOB were a school, well, the freaks and geeks were in study hall all day while I was out at recess. They had to sit there in a darkened room for their entire shift, staring at a screen that was projecting satellite imagery.

I sat down near one of the analysts, a Hispanic guy by the name of Hernandez. I knew that he was the best down-and-distance guy up there—he specialized in being able to determine the height of a building based on the shadow it cast and other means.

"Hernandez, I'm wondering if I need the ten-footer or the twenty to get up on there."

I put my finger on the screen, showing him which building I was referring to. As soon as my finger touched down, I could feel Tony cringing.

"My bad," I said, apologizing for the smudge.

He squinted for a minute and then said, "That's plus or minus twenty-five."

I figured we could use the aluminum collapsible ladder instead of the folding one.

"And what's the difference in height between this outer perimeter wall and this objective?"

A few seconds later I had my answer and knew that plan A wasn't going to work out. There was no way we could shoot over that wall. We wouldn't be able to see into that doorway from ground level. Tony ran me a bunch of other numbers and brought up several different views on screen.

He pointed at the screen, careful not to touch it, and said, "This building gives you the optimal sight picture of that doorway. If your focus is that objective in that part of the compound, then that's your spot."

I nodded and bumped fists with him. "Thanks so much."

I felt goose bumps prickling my skin as I made my way into the briefing room. I shook my head. I knew I wasn't fully dressed, but damn, that room was always so cold. Somebody kept the AC blasting in there, maybe because they figured once the room was filled with, say, forty guys, the body heat would build up. True to its name, the briefing was brief, just the squad leaders telling each of their guys, and the larger group, what their roles were going to be and what they'd be carrying. Just as important, we gave our call signs, the identifying names we'd use during our radio transmissions.

Weapons squad was going to be carrying the Carl Gustav recoilless rifle, basically a bazooka normally used to fire antitank missiles. I thought they were cool because they could fire nearly anything. Hell, you could shove a Crock-Pot in there and turn it into a deadly projectile.

I quickly filled the guys in on my call sign, where we were going to position ourselves, and when I was likely to break off from their element. Timing was critical but things seldom went exactly as planned. Still, it was important to keep that time factor in mind.

I love the sound of Velcro. I don't know what the military did before it was invented. Hearing thirty-five or so guys strapping stuff on with that simple hook and loop mechanism, the sound of tape being unrolled as guys secure things to keep as silent as possible, was like the music we'd play in the locker room before a game to get pumped up. That collective sound signaled that we all had each other's back. It wasn't the same strapping on your kit when you were alone; somehow that song came out tinny and uninspired.

The last little ritual was the burn barrel—a literal metal barrel where we destroyed any sensitive documents. No way we were going to risk letting any intel or operational directives fall into enemy hands. After the comms check was complete and the tech squared away anybody who was having trouble, it was go time. Pardon the pun, but radio failures happened with alarming frequency. You could use a radio one day set to a specific frequency and have no problems, and in the next operation, using the same frequency settings, it was like that radio forgot how to be a radio. The techs did the best they could, but as advanced as our technology was, what seemed a simple device often created problems and frustrations.

That night, maintaining radio discipline was almost impossible. Almost as soon as we were inserted, we started taking gunfire.

We'd been inserted via helicopter about two clicks from our objective. We walked along what I came to think of as waffle roads—narrow strips of packed dirt with ditches on each side, some of them intersecting at right angles. But instead of butter and maple syrup in those low-lying zones, raw sewage trickled and pooled. I clenched my teeth and hoped that I could control my gag reflex.

After what seemed like just a couple of minutes into the march toward the objective, we took enemy fire coming at us from eleven o'clock. They were laying down what should have been suppressive fire, but it was too scattered to really call it that. They'd fire a few bursts, we'd drop down into those divots and ditches, and then move on. We repeated that pattern four more times, each time dealing with slightly more intense fire, but in my mind it was like hiking through the woods and being swarmed by no-see-ums, those little bugs that irritated but didn't do any real damage.

The point guy was doing his thing, using his GPS to guide us through the dark. I was always amazed that the point man would walk with his eyes glued to his device, making sure that he was getting good updates from the GPS. The other guys around him were his eyes, helping him to navigate around, over, and through things that he could see only on his display.

By the time we got to the compound, I was ready for this one to be over. I liked being the shooter, but I hated being the target. Fortunately, we hadn't taken any casualties except for some shattered nerves. Once inside the wall, Pemberton and I broke off. I would have had to be blind to not spot the building Hernandez and I had discussed. It was the tallest in the village, and once I got up to it, I realized it was also one of the more impressive structures I'd come across in my desert deployments.

So many of the structures in Iraq and Afghanistan, unless you were in a major city, appeared to be hastily built, like they were sandcastles that could easily crumble when a ladder was leaned against their flanks. In this case, I heard a deep and satisfying thud when I placed my ladder. I looked up, and through my night vision the ladder seemed to glow, like highway lane dividers on a dark stretch of interstate.

Hernandez had been right about the building. It was

about twenty-five feet tall, and that meant my ladder was nearly vertical. If I shifted my weight backward at all, I'd come flying down onto my back. That would not be good at all. I wasn't sure if I was going to be able to climb back down, but as long as I got myself up there, that was all that mattered.

Once on top of the building, I checked in with Pemberton. I'd sent him over to another building so he could watch our six. I figured that the Taliban guys were going to come after us harder once they figured out that we were stationary.

Before he could reply, I heard a few pops from the line guys. I couldn't figure out what they were shooting at. I ran to the ledge and turned on my PVS-26 night-vision optics and my lasers. Beneath me was a thick canopy of trees, making it hard to get a good visual on the whole compound. Off comms, I could hear Pemberton yelling something, but I couldn't make him out clearly. After a few seconds, that didn't matter. Below me, I saw a man wearing a long blue shirt, white pants, and sandals, his long hair and beard black against the rest of his body. He was zigzagging along, taking cover in various places, moving with a sureness in the dark that made it seem like he'd preplanned every move on this chessboard.

The sound of Pemberton's Win Mag thundered and echoed and my vision went fuzzy, like the whole place had been shaken. The man froze in his tracks and I could see bark and tree shrapnel flying, just inches in front of the guy. If Pemberton was firing a warning shot, he just released a damn good one.

I looked to my three o'clock where the weapons squad had set up a blocking position. The man was running toward them, and it seemed like every one of his steps was punctuated by the sound of the M4s going after him. When the guy reached for his chest, my worst suspicions were confirmed. The guy was a suicide bomber and he was reaching to detonate his vest. Then he dashed into some heavy brush, and I knew at that point Pemberton wouldn't have eyes on him anymore. No way he could burn through that thick brush no matter how good his scope was.

The line guys had fired a bunch of rounds, but the man was still ticking. I could hear rounds rustling the branches and leaves, a stuttering weed-whacking kind of sound. No shouts from the Taliban guy, no sound that he'd been hit.

I was still breathing hard from the climb up to my position, so I went down to one knee. I detected movement; the target was now weaving among the trees again. I was able to put my crosshairs on him right in the center of his back as he moved away from me. I cranked my elevation knob down to one for a hundred-yard shot. I approximated that I'd be shooting from about a thirty-five-degree angle. I did some other quick calculations while tracking the guy. He was in a pretty good sprint, so I was holding about a half-mil distance in front of him to allow for that. I squeezed off a round. Because I wasn't a stable platform while being on one knee, the gun rose up and then settled back down so that I could see through the scope again.

"Crap. I missed," I muttered.

The man stopped and I immediately knew that he'd felt that bullet go by him. Most likely, I'd over-led him by a fraction. I backed off the lead some, my scope's crosshairs tattooing him on his right shoulder blade. I figured he was now about fifty meters away from the weapons squad, close enough to do some damage to them if he blew himself up.

I took a long, deep breath, easing out every bit of tension and oxygen in my body. As the gun settled back in, I shut my eyes for an instant. When I opened them again, the sight was right where I wanted it to be. I squeezed the trigger and the man disappeared from my view.

In an instant all the other gunfire fell silent.

I heard a high-pitched ecstatic voice come over the comms. "You got him! You got him!"

The weapons squad leader reported that they were going to search the man, strip him, and do the other assessments.

My heart was racing and I lowered the weapon and then sat down fully on the roof. Over the comms, I heard the weapons squad guys.

"Holy shit," somebody muttered.

I wondered what the hell was going on, what they'd found.

The weapons squad leader called me up on the comms.

"Roger that, Irv. You got him. He had a Russian grenade on him. I guess he was trying to get as close to us as he could."

I got back into position, knowing that the area wasn't fully secure, all the time thinking, "Thank God I got him with that second shot."

Later, once the area was secure, I climbed down. A cluster of weapons squad guys were looking at the back of a digital camera.

Calvert, a tall, wiry E5 with a gap-toothed grin and a movie-trailer narrator's voice, came up to me and offered his hand. "Damn. What a shot. When we walked up on the guy, I thought he was pissing the bushes. We knew the guy was hit, we heard the impact and him grunting and then going down, so we were all, like, what was that?"

The squad leader came over. "The bullet impacted him just below the shoulder, slightly off center middle back. The hollow point expanded and pushed everything up and out of his chest. His heart was hanging there on the outside of his body cavity, still pumping a couple of times, spraying the trees and leaves."

He offered me the camera he was carrying. I immediately fixated on the man's eyes, how glazed over they seemed and how his mouth hung open in surprise, like he understood what had just happened to him. I didn't want to deal with my thoughts about what I'd just done, so I immediately turned to Pemberton on the extraction.

"Dude, you suck so bad. A .300 Win Mag, a straight shot, and you missed?"

"Yeah, right. I had him nailed. Hit a frickin' tree limb and it deflected an inch."

I knew what he was saying was true. His round did have to penetrate some thick brush and trees.

"You don't hear me talking about being on one knee, in the dark, on a roof."

We continued like that even after we'd boarded the helicopter.

Over the open comms I heard several of the commanders say, "Good job, Irv. You're batting a thousand."

I said thanks, but later that night, just before racking out, I said to Pemberton, "What does batting a thousand mean?"

Pemberton gave me that dog look, cocking his head and staring at me. "You serious, dude? Baseball. Every time up you get a hit, you're batting a thousand. This is unbelievable. Two for two, well, really three for three since you got two the first night. This doesn't happen very often. Hell, maybe not ever."

I didn't realize it was such a big deal until the next day when we went to grab some chow midday. Perkins and Julian, another spotter-sniper pair, came up to us. They asked about whether it was true.

I showed them the photo.

"Man, this is stupid," Perkins said, running his hand

through his hair. The veins in his forehead were standing out like rivers on a relief map.

Julian just stood there staring at the picture, shaking his head. Finally he straightened and looked at the ceiling. "We haven't gotten out once, and you—How are you getting trigger time every op?"

"It's only been two days. I have no idea," I said. I was feeling pretty proud of getting the job done. I knew that it was luck of the draw, but still, these guys were really pissed off, just as I would have been if I was in their shoes. We were as competitive as could be, and I didn't take their brotherly hatred personally.

I wasn't going to let them off the hook easily and say that things could change the next day. I had a feeling that a different tempo was being established. I told myself that I had to be prepared for what was going to come next.

3. Misfires, Malfunctions, and Misery

"You've got four hot bodies on a rooftop firing over a short ledge," the third squad's leader, Sergeant Brooks, said over the comms. He was receiving reports from the AC-130 Spectre gunship that was flying overhead.

That explained why none of us had been shot to that point. We were basically in a shooting gallery. The bazaar in the center of the village was like an open tube preventing us from moving laterally. All the Taliban guys had to do was aim down the length of that tube and they could have shredded us. Instead, they were most likely just holding their guns over the lip of that low retaining wall on the rooftop, keeping their bodies behind it for protection, and essentially firing blind. Grateful that we weren't facing anyone with more discipline than that, I continued to low-crawl past other elements of our platoon until Pemberton and I reached the lead squad. That small group of six all fixed their wide eyes on us, and their expressions said it all. We were pinned down, and the only way to get out of this mess was to take out those guys on the rooftop. Eventually one of those guys might get lucky and one of us would end up being unlucky.

I looked back at Pemberton, and nodding to each side to indicate the rest of the guys, I said, "Roger that."

We lined up and got down in the lowest prone position we could and I turned on my flood. I adjusted my scope, cranking it all the way down until it bottomed out. I had a pretty close shot, about a hundred meters. So, after cranking it all the way down, I looked through it. I pulled my head back in disgust. All I saw was a bright white ball. Even though we were in the village, there was still a lot of vegetation and most of the infrared light I was shining was reflecting off it and back into my scope.

"Oh, crap, I can't see anything. Pemberton—I want you to use that .300 Win-Mag and I don't care if you hit the very base of the ledge of the rooftop, that bullet will punch right through. Just start putting heavy rounds down there until I get up on a knee and sort things out."

He manipulated the bolt, chambered a round, and squeezed. Then I heard the loudest click I've ever heard. I call it the click of death.

I looked at him, my expression asking him, Dude, how do you not have a round loaded in your gun? He looked up at me, nodding his head viciously, telling me, Yes I do.

Frustrated and angry, I shouted, "Dude, you don't have a round in there. What the f--k?"

I could hear bullets whining past us and impacting on the stone walls.

"I swear to freakin' God, there's one in there. I chambered and checked before."

Frustrated, angry, and a little bit scared that this mess-up could cause problems big-time, Pemberton and I continued fighting our own little verbal war while all hell was breaking loose around us. My mind was racing. Here we are, our third mission in with these guys, and we've suddenly gone from heroes to idiots.

"For the last freaking time," I yell at him, "load it back up."

He did as instructed and I watched a bullet pop out. Holy crap, he did have one in there. Maybe it was a dud or something. He went for it again and the same thing happened.

We both looked at each other in disbelief. His gun was out of commission. It must've got banged up in the incoming. Who knows? A grain of sand could've got inside his bolt carrier and not allowed the firing pin to fully strike the tail end of the bullet.

That's why I didn't like using bolt guns overseas. That kind of mechanical failure is pretty typical with bolt-action rifles because the bolt's open for so long. A lot of stuff can get in it. You've got to be supervigilant about cleaning and maintaining it. It has a really fine trigger, too. If the smallest grain of dirt gets in there, it screws up the whole rifle.

"*Okay, roger that*," I think. Now what?

When that beeper went off back at the base, I couldn't have imagined we'd find ourselves in that situation.

I don't know a whole lot about baseball, but when Pemberton explained to me what batting a thousand meant, I immediately thought that it was impossible to go a whole season never making an out. Call me a pessimist, though most likely I'm just a realist, but I knew that our run of good fortune wasn't likely to continue. I had a sense that we were going to see a lot of action, and as much as I was confident in our abilities, there are too many variables that go into successful sniping to think that we could continue to have the kind of takeout rate we were enjoying. Besides, I'd reasoned, two nights was too small of a sample to draw any real conclusions from.

Having my spotter, a good shooter as well, go down with a weapon malfunction was just the war gods' way of telling us not to get too comfortable.

In the immediate, I was really pissed at Pemberton, though later on I'd come to my senses and realize that stuff like that happens. It wasn't a human-error failure, not directly, but a mechanical one. Stuff breaks down. Iraq and Afghanistan are harsh environments in which to operate. I had to remind myself that getting pissed off and losing focus wasn't going to help the situation one bit.

Besides, I'd had my share of times when I was the one

who had screwed up, or narrowly escaped a screwup. Things have a way of evening themselves out.

Late in 2005, just before my first deployment, I had one of the worst training cycles I've ever had and maybe any Ranger has ever had. We were at Fort Benning training to do an airport seizure. We were in a C-17, packed in there in total darkness along with some Humvees, some little birds, and a few of the minimotorcycles that Chuck Norris had used in the movie *Delta Force*. I thought those were so cool.

I sat there with my rucksack, assault pack, and my 203 grenade launcher. When the time came to go, I stood up, hooked into the overhead cables, and waited in line. After I jumped, I did my four count. Nothing. Five count. Nothing still. I looked up and could see my parachute was in a cigarette roll—just a long, slim strand of fabric. That's what we call a partial malfunction. I'm hurtling along, the wind screaming in my ears, flying past guys who've had successful deployments.

They were screaming at me, "Pull your reserve! Pull your reserve!"

I did exactly that, and the reserve billowed out. Somehow, though, my leg got caught underneath the riser, so I was coming down in this funky position. My left foot was up near my helmet and it was like I was doing the splits. I was trying to steer the reserve—which was impossible since the reserve is a nonsteerable device—and I looked down and saw I was maybe a hundred fifty to two hundred feet above the concrete runway. I knew I was descending too rapidly, and I was only going to have just a single leg to land on, but there wasn't much I could do at that point.

I hit the ground hard and rolled over while being dragged along the ground by the chute. My equipment was being thrown off me, I could smell rubber from the soles of my boot dragging along, and I finally came to rest. I tried to hop up immediately. This was my first jump in battalion, and I'd managed to make it into a what-not-to-do film.

Truth is, the first thought I had right before impact was, "My mom's going to kill me."

The rest of my guys came running over to me to make sure that I was okay. I didn't want to let on that my knee hurt like hell. I told everybody I was okay and drove on. Later, after the exercise was over, I was taken to the medical center and, fortunately, everything checked out. I had a badly swollen knee, a few bumps and bruises, but I was okay.

Maybe I shouldn't have done this, but I called my mom and told her about what happened. Despite her army background she said, "Why in the world do they have you jumping out of airplanes anyway? That makes no sense. That's not a very safe job for you."

Funny thing was, she seemed better about me being deployed—a few tears and hugs and requests that I call whenever possible, that was about it. Every time she knew that I had a jump on my schedule, she'd always call to check in, telling me how nervous she'd been all day worrying about me.

I have to admit that even though that incident sounds a lot like Pemberton's—an equipment failure—I was responsible for what happened.

I have a huge fear of heights. I was able to overcome it in jump school to some extent, but my nerves got the best of me that night. I was heavily loaded with gear, and I wondered how that was going to affect my aerodynamics and everything else. I was thinking too much, so when it came time to jump, I kind of tumbled out and the extra weight and my poor jump combined to have me rolling from the start. I got all tangled up in the risers as I was tumbling in the air.

The first sergeant and platoon sergeant were good about making sure I was okay, but the next day we had an incident review. They showed me the video of my exit and all that did was reinforce what I already knew. I essentially blacked out on the exit. If I had waited another few seconds before deploying the reserve, they would have had to use a shovel and a mop to clean me off the concrete.

I could have been reprimanded far worse than I was. Instead I was assigned extra jump training. I must have put my gear on and off dozens of time, doing practice exits over and over. I knew that the army didn't want to see anyone fail, and it was better to get training than punishment.

Truth is, though, I should have never been in that position. I'd done my airborne school training, had done so many PLFs (parachute landing falls), and had spent so much time on the T-10 Delta parachutes working those risers that I began to wonder if maybe I was a puppet, that I should have performed better that first time with battalion.

One thing about all that training I went through, first at basic then at Airborne and later at RIP and beyond, it made me face reality. I'd fantasized about being a soldier for so long, and I'd built up this image of who I was and what I was capable of, but when faced with some of the tasks I had to complete, that image wasn't as accurate as I'd hoped. I had always thought of myself as an adrenaline junkie/thrill seeker. However, standing on a tower nearly thirty-five feet or so up in the air and having to walk across a narrow balance beam to another tower that seemed to be a mile away was almost enough to get me to quit. Later, in Ranger school, the zip line over water also had me thinking that it would be better to just walk away and disqualify myself than give myself a heart attack or panic attack in the middle of the exercise.

I figured out pretty quickly that the reality of life in the military was tougher than I'd imagined. In basic, I saw a couple of guys run off and one guy who broke down so completely that he slit his wrists in a bathroom stall. He survived, as did the few other knuckleheads who tried to break their legs jumping off the top bunk. Getting through basic was easy physically, but mentally it was tough. We had fifty guys in a barracks and the rumors were constantly flying about what was going to happen to us. We had guys trying to hurt or kill themselves and it seemed like everyone we worked with was trying to break us down. We had to go through the "racetrack"—a chow line punishment where you had to eat as much as you could in the time it took to get food on your tray and walk the twenty feet to the garbage can—more times than I can remember.

In some ways, my eagerness to become a soldier ended up hurting me, literally, in the long run. I'd rented some Navy SEAL training DVDs and was doing a lot of running in boots—combat boots. Later, at the end of basic when it came time to do the running qualifications, I had developed such serious stress fractures that I was held back for a few weeks to heal up. We were a Christmas Exodus class, so we had two weeks off. I went home and woke up each morning with painfully swollen legs. I started to think that maybe I'd made a mistake in choosing the military as a career.

I also thought I could outsmart the system and that eventually backfired. My dad had taught me how to make my bed in the military style when I was in my early teens. By the time I got to basic, I was a master at it. The first time we ever had a bed inspection, I was singled out by the drill sergeant for my exemplary work. Figuring why mess with success, I decided not to sleep in the bed again. I'd sleep on top of the sheets and blanket, or I'd sleep under the bed frame on the floor, but I would not get *in* the bed. A few other guys saw what I was doing and copied my example.

That did not sit well with Sergeant Fredley, the scariest man I'd ever met. He was only about five three or five four. He never raised his voice, but he was a weird dude. He'd wake us up in the middle of the night, tell us what clothes to put on—sometimes our Class A shoes, a ball cap, a tie, and a T-shirt—and make us form up outside. We'd stand there for half an hour and then he'd say, "Okay. That's it. Back to bed." He reminded me in some ways of Hannibal Lecter, that eerie kind of in-control evil.

When he found out about guys not sleeping in their beds so they didn't have to remake them every night, he put us through some hellacious PT, never once raising his voice, just giving us that weird glassy-eyed stare.

In truth, I probably tortured myself more than anyone else did. I had been dating a girl all of my senior year of high school. I was head over heels for her, and I thought she was for me. Jay was into me, but not that into me as it turned out. I think my parents cried tears of joy when I went off to basic and had to leave her. I had a part-time job working at a shoe store and every bit of money I earned went to the care and support of Jay. I didn't know the expression "high maintenance" back then, but that was what Jay was. All through basic, I wrote her a letter every day, but I didn't get a single one back. I was eighteen and fragile at that point. I came up with all kinds of reasons why I wasn't getting any mail from her. The drill sergeants were stealing my letters was the final conclusion I came to. To support that idea, the drill sergeants used to sing this song. The lyrics went, "Jody's got your girl back home." The gist of the song was that you are away in basic and now someone else was taking care of her. I'm ashamed to admit it now, but I had to fight back tears whenever I heard them singing that song.

Finally, when I got back home for Christmas, my best friend Andre and I went to her high school to surprise her. Of course, I saw her and she was holding some other guy's hand, walking out to his car in the parking lot. I went nuts and ran up to her yelling at her. Andre, who was more like a brother than a friend, really went after her, defending me and telling her how she didn't deserve a great guy like me.

Later, on the last day before I had to return to finish basic, Andre was in my room. I had my bags packed and he grabbed them and threw them around, telling me that I didn't have to go back. He said that he didn't want me to have to go to war. I told him not to worry about that, but I did have some serious second thoughts about what I was doing. I had a great family, a really good friend, and what was I giving all that up for? Obviously, I did go back, but five more guys out of our original fifty didn't show up. Ultimately, my pride kicked in. I'd been telling people for so long that I wanted to be a soldier, that I couldn't imagine going back home and having to live down that failure to follow through. It also helped that my dad was firm but sympathetic. He told me he understood how I felt and that he'd support me a hundred percent, but he'd hate to see me make a bad decision that I'd have to live with for the rest of my life. He told me that quitting is addictive and that it got easier and easier to do each time you made that decision. That was advice I was glad I took to heart.

I also think that part of what contributed to that jump accident was my eagerness to deploy for the first time. I'd wanted to be a soldier for so long and the initial training phases seemed to drag on for so long. I enjoyed learning as much as I did, but I was tired of practicing all the time—I wanted to be doing it for real.

I can't say that there was a single incident that transformed me from fearful to eager. Over time, doing all the training, receiving guidance from fellow soldiers and higher-ups made me more and more certain that I was doing what I wanted and was meant to do. I laugh now thinking of it, but when I went to the army recruiting station, I asked for a twenty-year contract.

The recruiter looked at me and said, "I'm impressed by your willingness to commit, but you should think about that for a bit. Twenty years is a very long time."

"I know that, but I'm sure that I'll be good to go for all that time."

Eventually he talked me down a bit. Quite a bit, actually.

I signed for a guaranteed six and a half years. I told my recruiter that it didn't matter, I was going to do the full twenty anyway.

I'm sure that if you talked to the men and women who work in those recruitment positions, they'll have plenty of other stories about overeager and gung-ho types like me. Reality sets in quickly, and some people it frightens away and other people it hardens to the task at hand. Sometimes hardness makes you brittle and more likely to crack.

Sometimes what you need is somebody to help you push through to find out that the limits you thought you had were just a little beyond your expectations of yourself. Sometimes you fall short of what you thought you were capable of, but then someone gives you the push you need to accept that limitations are temporary things.

My leg issues—the stress fractures—almost proved to be too much for me. The last evolution in basic was an FTX or field exercise. A guy by the name of Lloyd came to my aid and helped me on the last bit of the fourteen-mile road march. He knew I was struggling and took some of the stuff out of my rucksack and carried it the rest of the way to the finish line. In some ways, I was like this bike we had back in the neighborhood. We lived on a cul-de-sac and we used to race this bike around that circle. It was the fastest bike out there it seemed like, no matter who was riding it. But it didn't have brakes. A couple of buddies from the street got hit while riding Speedy Gonzales because they couldn't slow down when a car was coming. I guess that was kind of what I was like, only I got lucky and never got hit.

I was also fortunate that I struck up a relationship with a guy named Mark Cunningham. When I was still waiting for my first overseas deployment, he was already into his second and then third tour in Iraq and Afghanistan. He was only a year older than I was, but he was a pretty seasoned veteran in terms of his experience. I had taken advantage of my squad leader's experience and asked all kinds of questions about what to expect and what it was like over there. However, I didn't want to overstay my welcome with him, so to speak, and Cunningham always seemed fine with talking to me. He was from Tennessee, and a lot of times when guys told me they were from someplace other than the Northeast, I had a hard time picturing where that was. He was a good guy, had an ever-present dip of Copenhagen behind his lip, and was always patient with me.

What I knew about the war was what I'd seen on CNN or wherever. I was thinking we'd go over there and live in tents. I told the guys that and they all laughed at me. Cunningham always set me straight. He'd give me crap, but at least he'd laugh and tell me it was okay to ask and to not know things. Our informal briefings and debriefings helped me prepare for what really was unimaginable in so many ways.

That's not to say that all my various training schools and activities were horrible. I loved firing the rocket launchers. Getting qualified on them was fun. By the time I did so, I'd been in the army for a couple of years. I'd also gained a bunch of weight. Mom was a great cook but with four mouths to feed and not a whole lot of income, things got spread pretty thin. I was one of those guys in basic and after who seldom complained about the chow. It was a good thing I put on those twenty to twenty-five pounds, because the recoils of the 203 and M240B were so powerful, it would have bucked that skinnier me back into basic.

I never got to fire them in actual combat, but spending all day on the range watching those things spiral and twist downrange until they impacted was about as relaxing as anything I ever did. Seeing those eighteen-wheeler trucks roll up with thousands and thousands of rounds of ammo ready to be offloaded and fired was like Christmas Day for me.

Still, I made my share of mistakes early on and even later. Those bumps in the road were good to experience, even when one of those bumps was an M1-Abrams reinforcement tank of ours that I nearly fired on mistakenly during my first deployment in Iraq.

I guess you can say that trusting my gut wasn't something that came natural to me. But in this case, on that third night operation, maybe if I did trust my gut, I'd have thought to make sure that Pemberton and his weapon were truly squared away.

Even though we only had those two missions under our belt, things had gone so smoothly everybody's morale seemed to be up. Just walking around our area within the compound, you could sense that people were really into it in a different way. It's hard to say exactly how things were different, but people seemed to be moving at a different pace for one thing. It was like everybody had a designated time and location in mind. Instead of just killing time, we were moving around knowing that something was going to be up that night and we'd better be prepared for it.

Even in my earlier deployments, before becoming a sniper team leader, I'd gotten into the habit of hanging back when it was time to load up. That wasn't because I didn't like flying in the helicopters. Instead, it was a part of my desire to get out there. If I hung back on load-up, that meant I was going to be among the first out when we landed. I wasn't troubled by visions of us being ambushed and trapped inside that fuel-filled bird. I just knew that given my role as a sniper attached to this unit, if anything was going to go down early on, I wanted to be out there firing as close to on point as I could be. With our night-vision and thermal-imaging scopes, we were the eyes of the platoon, and there was no sense in having them be in the back of our heads— let alone the back of the bird.

Besides, I liked riding along with the dog and the dog handler. If we were the eyes of the platoon, those guys were the nose and whatever other sense it is that those dogs possess that tips them off that something could potentially go upside down before we even had a clue. Something in my gut told me that as by the book as this operation seemed during our briefing, something was going to disrupt those plans. I trusted my instincts as much as I trusted the animal's.

Forty-five minutes later, we touched down and offloaded. My earlier feelings about this not being a run-of-the-mill operation were confirmed. As soon as my feet hit the ground, I noticed two things. First, the full moon painted every bit of the location in a kind of primer-gray light. Our night-vision gear was going to be even more effective as a result. Second, we weren't going to be sneaking up on anybody. For the first time in my four deployments, the enemy was firing tracer rounds at us. Their green glow against the ash-gray backdrop reminded me of flickering Christmas lights. It was a surreal scene to have what seemed the entire galaxy above us bathing us in light while those tracers arced and flared in the distance.

We formed up and set off with the dog Bruno and his handler, Sergeant Val, on point. About a click or so in, we came on another small village, and we could make out a circle of bodies lying outside. We could hear some heavy breathing and snoring and saw a few of the bodies rising and falling as they breathed in their sleep. I felt bad for Sergeant Val and even worse for Bruno. Bruno was trained to go after the bad guys and bite them to bring them under control, and his every instinct and training was telling him to seek and bite. Collectively, we made our way through the sleepers, figuring that the direct route was best. We entered the village marketplace. Bazaar was a good name for that location since I was always freaked out about moving along and through them at night. The small buildings all had garage door–like entrances, and they were recessed just enough to resemble cave entrances, providing who knows who with a good hiding place.

Besides Taliban fighters, the doorways could also be hiding IEDs. The dog led the way, his tail high and twitching, his snout high and sniffing. Eventually, I lost sight of him. The first and second squads moved ahead of Pemberton and me to do the clearing.

We had gone about thirty-five of the fifty meters we had to navigate to reach our destination when a green tracer round appeared ahead of me. I ducked and heard it sizzle past, like a bottle rocket the kids in the neighborhood used to fire at one another. It seems like a cliché to say this, but I saw all this happening in slow motion—the light wobbling as it fireballed toward me, giving off sparks of light. It was almost pretty the way it lit up the gray night. Fortunately, my brain wasn't working in slo-mo, and I dropped to one knee and a few more tracers went over my head.

Pemberton was just behind and flanking me and we both dropped to our bellies.

In our earpieces, we were getting transmissions from the AC-130 gunships patrolling above us. Ignoring their words for a moment, I told Pemberton, "Let's go," and we low-crawled. By this time, the rest of the guys in the platoon had opened fire; the Taliban's tracers were originating from a rooftop between one hundred fifty and two hundred meters away.

We continued our low crawl to the front of the formation. The rest of the guys were laying down a lot of lead, but they weren't hitting any of the targets. From experience, I knew that using a laser and an M4, trying to hit targets that were popping up just barely high enough that their eyeballs were visible for only an instant was going to make for a very difficult shot. Shortly after that, we discovered that Pemberton's gun wasn't going to be able to get it done either. I thought for a few seconds and then spoke to Mike.

"Put your flood on the target and I'll turn mine off."

"Roger that."

I knew I needed illumination, but I didn't need to have my scope refracting and reflecting all that light directly back into my eye. With him flooding from a different angle, I should have been able to avoid that problem.

When Pemberton's light went on, I saw a circle of light nearly six feet around tracing the perimeter of the rooftop

ledge. Through my scope I saw what I was hoping to see—
the whites of the Taliban guys' eyes glowing in the dark. If
you've ever been near a dog and seen how a light reflects off
their eyes, then you can imagine to some extent what I was
seeing. As I was looking, the white-eye glow went off and
on as the men blinked.

They stopped firing at us. Thirty seconds to a minute
passed. Blinking and silence.

"Hold the light right there. I'm going to take that guy
out first."

"Roger that."

"I'm going to keep moving to the right and work my way
from left to right."

"Got it."

Pemberton knew what to do. As I fired each round, he
was going to move the light along the row of eyeballs.

I squeezed the trigger and saw a large puff of smoke
through my scope. Low. I hit the wall and not the dude.

I reached up on my elevation and went up two clicks on
the gun, two minutes. That way I had given myself a bit of
leeway. Either I was going to hit the very top of his head
and crease his skull or hit him right between the eyes. I
reset the trigger and felt and heard the little click. I wanted
to reduce the pull. That was crucial for such a precise shot,
particularly with the two-stage trigger my weapon employed.

An instant after I squeezed the trigger, I saw the target's

eyes roll back just as his head first tilted straight back and then plunged forward like his head was on a spring.

I thought I'd hit him, but it was only when I heard a splash on the ground, what sounded like a chunky liquid being spilled, that I was more or less certain the round had found its mark. Nearly simultaneously with the sound, I saw Pemberton moving to my left as he brought his floodlight onto the second of the four men in line. That next target ducked below the ledge. For the next few seconds, I was reminded of the Whac-A-Mole game at Chuck E. Cheese's as the three remaining heads popped up at irregular intervals and locations.

Each time a head came up, I fired another round, taking that guy out. After the second, I could hear a few of our guys on comms laughing.

"You're getting them, Irv!" Lindley said. "This is unf'ing-real!" I recognized Lindley by his signature expression.

I was gaining confidence and feeling pretty good about getting these guys. They'd been making our lives miserable for a while. Now it was our time to return the favor.

After the third guy had gone down, I fired another round, hoping to end things, but I missed. I could make out a figure on all fours crawling away from us, just a hairline of his lower back visible above the wall. No way I could make that shot. No way I wanted that guy to get away.

Torres was positioned to Pemberton's left, the barrel of

his grenade launcher barely poking above his helmet. He was maybe six feet away from me.

"Torres, dude, you've got to launch one of those directly behind the building. Let him know that he's got no place to run."

Torres nodded and brought the weapon into firing position. Before I could tell him to wait, I felt concussive pressure stuffing my ears. Every sound went muffled and it felt like someone had taken a huge pair of pliers to my head.

I was pissed, but I knew that it was my own fault. No one had told me to not wear my ear protection. That was my choice and now I was paying for it. I was notorious for not using those foam earplugs because they were a distraction when I was concentrating on a target.

I instantly felt bad for jumping Torres's ass, but I couldn't take the words back. We still had to eliminate that target, and I had no time to answer Torres's puzzled look.

I don't know if it was the sound of the explosion that broke the last guy's discipline or if he tired as he moved farther away from the near wall, but he seemed to rise up a bit, exposing most of his back to me. I knew that a shot to the spine would incapacitate him immediately. I reaimed and squeezed off another round and watched as the body went flat on the roof and lay still.

I looked over toward Pemberton who was still holding the flood. Next to him, Brett looked at me and flashed a thumbs-up.

I nodded and said, "That was pretty cool."

"Sure was," Brett said, "but I got shot."

"Are you serious?"

"I am, but the damage isn't." He held up his hand and I could see a thin trickle of blood going from the meat on the outside of his palm tracking down his wrist.

Brett had already earned a Purple Heart when a Stryker he was riding in was blown up in Iraq during a previous deployment we were both on.

"I just got nicked. Don't say anything."

I knew that he didn't want any attention for that wound because he might get put up for a medal or citation.

I kept my mouth shut about Brett's wound, but I told the rest of the guys that we'd continue toward our objective. First, I wanted to mount the building where the Taliban guys had been. Once I could verify that things were clear, the guys could proceed a few blocks, Pemberton and I would hop onto the next building, and we'd kind of piggyback our way until we could get to our primary target.

Pemberton was still pretty upset about his weapon not firing, so I gave him some time to work on it while we were on the roof.

"I can't freakin' believe this shit. Third mission and I look like a piece of shit in front of everybody."

"I know, it sucks." I was looking through my scope, making sure the area was clear. I didn't want to turn around and look at Pemberton. "We'll get back home and we'll figure it out. We'll work something out so that this doesn't happen again."

A few minutes of silence followed. Then I could hear Pemberton muttering something. I thought he was talking to himself, but when I listened closer, I realized he was talking to one of the corpses.

"When you woke up this morning, I bet you didn't think this was how your day was going to turn out. Well, I didn't either."

I thought that was true for the rest of us as well. We'd still made little progress toward our initial objective, covering maybe one of the five clicks we had to cover. We'd taken fire immediately, been pinned down by four guys, and we were still making our way cautiously forward, about as slowly as we'd ever moved.

I took a second to look back at Pemberton to see how he was doing. Sure enough, his back was against the wall and he was talking to one of the dead guys.

"This is ridiculous." Pemberton let out a big sigh and shook his head and kind of chuckle-snorted.

I'd seen the dead guy's eyes just staring straight ahead. They were what gave away his exact position, what I'd used as a frame of reference through my scope, and they were still revealing things. He was dead. We weren't. It couldn't have been more simple or more complex.

As soon as we caught up with the rest of the squad, we encountered more enemy fire.

"Now," I said. "Now, *this* is ridiculous."

We established a defensive perimeter and Keyes and the rest of first and second squad were laying waste to our attackers with their MK-48s and M4s. Those belt-fed machine guns are nice and light at a little over eighteen pounds and they can fire 500 to 625 rounds a minute. Whoever those guys were that took us on were hopelessly outgunned with their AKs.

I wasn't feeling sorry for those guys at all. I saw one of the Taliban combatives hiding in the bush. He had his back to us and he was hunched over. I watched him through the scope. Something caught the moonlight and reflected back in the objective lens of my scope. I could see that he had some kind of radio, nothing more than a little walkie-talkie but it could still do us harm.

It was weird to have this intense firefight going on and, in the middle of it, kind of in a no-man's-land, this solitary guy. I didn't know if he was communicating with the other dudes or if that device could trigger some explosives. Didn't matter. He had to go down.

While I was watching him, he turned slightly and the barrel of his AK glinted off my infrared light, almost like sparks.

I turned to Pemberton. "You want this guy."

"I got him."

Again the death click.

I could see that Pemberton wanted to bite through the barrel of that Win Mag.

I shrugged and then aimed and took the guy out.

By this time the line guys were moving forward doing what they were supposed to do. You don't want to just stay in one spot when ambushed. I could see that they'd already gone past the feet of the dead dudes.

Things had quieted for a bit. Those firefights are more like match fights. They lasted about as long as a couple of kitchen matches take to burn out. Some of the squad members were taking the enemies' weapons, others clearing buildings. I was checking the rooftops and, in looking up, I could see that the sun was starting to creep up over the horizon. I couldn't believe that much time had passed.

Once we got within a click or two of the objective, Pemberton and I and the members of the third squad, broke off from the main element. We had to cross a narrow ravine. Fortunately there was a bridge we could use to cross it. It was just a narrow piece of lumber, no wider than a two-by-four, so we had to cross one at time. That meant that the six squad guys and then Pemberton and I would go over. We couldn't risk walking it, so we had to straddle the plank and kind of hunch our way across. While waiting my turn, I looked over my shoulder. I could hear gunfire and could see rounds impacting the building behind where our remaining element was.

I'd been on dozens and dozens of operations, but I'd never seen anything like this. I started wondering where the heck we were. Was every Taliban fighter in the country gathered in Helmand Province?

It was my turn to cross, and I about fell off when I heard Mac start screaming. Talk about a hard-charging Ranger. That was Mac. At first I couldn't figure out what he was hollering about, but when his banshee shriek kept up, I knew he was just pumping himself and the other guys up.

When he finally put words to his shouts, yelling, "Get some," in a throat-tearing tone, I smiled.

"Let's do what the man says," I told Pemberton.

We broke off from the squad into a spot behind a low stone wall. I wanted to observe the firefight through my scope to surveil them in case some random guy popped up again and tried to take out some of the guys in contact. I heard a high-pitched wail, not human this time, and then saw a huge cloud of sparks and dirt rise dangerously close to the main element. In the light, I could see our guys hunkered down behind a big wood and metal plow and a wheelbarrow, while around them piles of dirt and rock were fluming into the air and landing not more than fifty to a hundred feet from their position.

That 105 howitzer round was right on target though. Through my scope, I saw a head and then a rifle. That rifle was attached to a body and that man and his weapon started to shoot. I had no idea who it was, but just like before, here was this lone guy seemingly in the middle of nowhere firing away. I was so in the moment, so in the fog of war, I instinctively slid my safety off. I slowly started to squeeze, taking the slack out of the trigger, when the head shifted position slightly and I saw light reflecting off it. I immediately lowered the weapon and released the tension on the trigger. Only our guys wore that kind of infrared reflective strip of tape on our helmets.

I rose to one knee and pinched the bridge of my nose until my head could clear. I tried to chase the thoughts out of my mind, but what if I hadn't seen that reflective glint until a second later? That really drove home something I knew but obviously needed reinforcing. Be a hundred percent sure that is exactly who you intend on shooting and have no doubt in your mind.

Pemberton and I pushed on to a little building about a hundred meters away from the original target. We got on top and began searching. The sky was getting lighter, the cows were lowing, and sure as shit, the locals were awake and coming outside. Bombs were being dropped, jets were flying overhead, gunfire was being exchanged, and all that noise and chaos was like a wake-up call for these people. I couldn't believe it. Only later did I realize that these villagers had been experiencing these kinds of things for the majority of their lives. Like people who live near railroad tracks or a busy highway or a fire station or whatever, all those sounds had just become white noise to them. Sad.

We were up on top of this building and we could hear

the C-4 getting strapped on, blowing up the main objective's building's front door. Later we learned that luckily for us, the guy was still in there. I don't know why he hadn't left like the rest of the people had. Get out of the house and get some fresh air?

I don't know if his leaving would have made a difference. Later on in the deployment my questions about why people chose to stay or leave got answered. It was because of the amount of firepower we had. We used every asset available—F-16 jets, AC-130 gunships, mortar rounds. With all that weaponry at our disposal, we present ourselves as a much larger threat. On the ground, we were a forty-man element, but with those guns in the air, it must have seemed like an entire battalion or two was just outside their doors. As one of my old football coaches used to say about some of the blitz packages we used—they won't know whether to shit or go blind. Simply put, confusion and chaos reigned and flight or fight got all jumbled up.

After the objective was somewhat secure, Pemberton and I stayed on the roof providing cover for the guys conducting a sensitive site exploitation (SSE). They examined all the stuff inside the house, looking for cell phones, documents, computers, hard drives, everything. Pemberton and I were surveying the surroundings making sure those guys were safe. Pemberton cracked open his bolt and started to fix his weapon again. I observed a bad guy popping his head around the corner. He was looking at us and I wondered, what's this guy doing? He was three hundred meters away. So I continued to watch him watch us. I could just see his eyes and forehead peeking around the corner. He'd go back behind the corner and slowly come back out. He did that about ten times as I continued scoping him.

I told Pemberton, "Dude, if this guy has a weapon and decides to come out, I want you to take him."

If his gun was working, I wanted Pemberton to get that experience of a three-hundred-yard shot—a pretty typical and average shot for a direct action sniper. I wanted him to take it. I'd had my share for that night. I wanted him to be a part of it and stop thinking like he screwed up big-time.

He put his bolt back in. "I'm going to try it, man."

By then, we'd been watching this guy for fifteen minutes, and for some reason he decided to get really cocky. He stood straight up and slowly started to walk out. He was walking really stiff. Only one arm was moving. We couldn't see his opposite arm.

Nobody walked like that unless they were carrying something or they're trying to hide something. Still, after what had just gone on, I wanted to be sure.

The man slowly pulled around his AK-47 and pointed it right at the building we were on.

This guy's got to be kidding me.

He cranked off a few rounds. Boom, boom, boom. I heard one snap and the other two rounds hit the building's side.

Pemberton was right on it. I was looking at the guy, spotting his round for him, when Pemberton hammered him. The guy spun around and dropped.

I looked at Pemberton with my mouth dropped open and my eyes wide. "That hurt so bad." I'd wanted to be able to hear everything and hadn't put in my ear protection once again.

That Win Mag, without a suppressor, produced such a noise that it felt like the building was still shaking seconds after the round was fired and that my brain was rattling around in my skull.

Pemberton was smiling this face-splitting grin, glad that his weapon was back in action and he'd gotten some on that operation. I was glad for him too.

After that, it was finally over. There'd be another time to look back on all the could-haves and might-haves and all the rest. For now, we just wanted to get the hell out of there. Though the sun coming up was usually a signal for people to get out of bed, we were dog tired and hungry and would put off going to bed until we ate. Mostly, though, we were glad we'd escaped without any serious casualties.

My hearing was getting back to normal; it no longer sounded like somebody had clamped a jar over each of my ears. That was a good thing because nothing beat the sound of victory, the chatter of a bunch of guys who'd gone out and done their jobs, erased their mistakes, and put a serious hurtin' on some guys.

4. A Ranger in the Making

After a really hectic few days, it was good to have two days off. I hadn't really been able to settle into my room yet. It was also good to have the time to get a better sense of where we were and what the reason was for things being so hot. Guys like to settle into a battle rhythm, but when you don't have any kind of a buildup, and are forced to hit the ground running, seemingly sprinting with no finish line in sight—or even mentioned—you get a bit worn down. You know, we're supposed to follow orders and do our jobs and just perform, but we're human beings and uncertainty isn't our friend.

Before my deployment to Afghanistan, I tried to keep up with what was going on there, but it wasn't like I had a lot more sources of information than a civilian would have—television news and newspapers. Of course, when guys came back, we'd talk to them about what they'd done, but it wasn't like we were conducting a State Department or Defense Department briefing regarding the overall battle plan and strategic maneuvering for the region. We were just guys doing a job and wanting to know what the chow was like, what kinds of operations they went on, the environmental conditions, that kind of thing.

As it turned out, the Helmand Province and the area in and around Kandahar was particularly important. The U.S. had never really maintained a large military presence there, from what I was told, and it was only after I returned from this deployment that news of a big push in the area came out. In fact, I was sitting on my couch watching CNN in September of 2009 when I heard that the U.S. was going to send the marines in there, and this was the first time since 2001 that the U.S. would have boots on the ground there. I sat back and laughed, thinking, *Wait a minute, didn't I just spend two and a half months right there?*

That's really when it started to make sense to me why the fighting was so fierce in that area. The place was a Taliban safe haven. A lot of the fighters who had fled from the action at the beginning of the war had made their way there. At the time, we were told that this was also the area from which up to ninety-eight percent of the opium, and eventually heroin, that enters the U.S. originates. The Taliban would use the profits of that sale to fund their terrorist activities. I remember thinking in those early days in the country when we were being so heavily fired on, from where the heck did these guys get all their armament?

We had a terrorism specialist as part of our unit, and he

was the one who told us about the ninety-eight percent and the heroin connection. I have to admit, that pissed me off a bit. I was out there laying my life on the line, along with all the other guys, and I believed that I was defending my country. Yet some of the people I was defending were buying an illegal drug that was in turn helping to buy the weapons these guys were using to try to kill me. We'd be walking along for miles and these opium poppy fields would just go on and on, and I kept thinking about how weird this place was and how confusing the whole situation was. I wanted to just forget about it, and most of the time I could, but in those down moments I would try to make sense of it all, even though it was nearly impossible to do so. I eventually figured out I wasn't the only who was struggling with all those thoughts.

So, in between those hours of debate, I did what I needed to do—I cleaned my weapon. Just before lunch hour for the regular guys, I'd sit out on the balcony having a smoke and cleaning my weapon before going to bed. Despite what happened on the previous assignment with Pemberton's weapon, I had to knock on Pemberton's door and ask him to join me to do weapons maintenance. I never issued him a direct order or pulled rank on him. He was six years older than me, and at the age of twenty-three, I still wasn't comfortable with outranking guys who were older than me. I believed that guys who were older and had more time in the army deserved respect, so I asked them not to call me "sergeant." My attitude was this was a stressful enough environment and we should be trying to enjoy our deployment as best we could. No point in wasting your breath saying "sergeant" all the time. We were going out every day getting shot at and our compound came under rocket fire daily. You could die any time, so why stick with those regulations and formality? I was Irv to my friends, so why shouldn't I be Irv to all these guys with whom I was sharing such an intense experience? I really believed in and tried to live the brothers-in-arms ideal.

I can admit now that I was a bit immature in some ways when I joined the army and I did some things that I'm really not proud of. Same was true before I enlisted. My parents told me that I was always trying to act like I was really mature, but by trying to do that, I was actually being just the opposite. Maybe it was just teenage hormones and all the changes you go through with puberty and all that, but at sixteen, I was just into doing stupid stuff, mild by some standards, but still enough to make my mom and dad wonder just exactly who I was and what the hell was going on with me.

I was on the Internet looking for ways to make weapons from household items and I came across instructions for a blowgun you could fashion out of a shoelace, a sewing needle, and a straw. I scavenged the supplies and spent a lot of time shooting that little dart around. Eventually, I got a bigger piece of pipe and a small nail and used that. I was surprised by how powerful the thing was. I shot a bottle of cologne I had and it started leaking. Then, I fired another shot and this one missed the target and hit my bedroom window. Andre was with me and he freaked out when he saw the glass shatter. It also tore up the outside screen pretty bad. I cleaned things up the best I could but my dad spotted the damage and asked me what happened. I was feeling pretty good about myself for coming up with what I thought was a great excuse (lie) that matched the laws of thermodynamics. It had gotten cold the night before and then the sun shining on the window heated up the glass again. I shut it and the glass broke.

He seemed to believe me, and all he asked was that I patch up the screen. He'd take care of the glass. I had to get a ladder and deal with the second-story window—that's when I discovered I was afraid of heights. I also discovered something else. My dad was a very cool guy and a very fair one. On the day I was to leave for basic he said to me, "Before you go, check your bank account's balance."

I asked him why.

"Because you'll see you've got a few dollars less than you probably thought. I took out the money I spent to fix that window you broke with your blowgun."

"How'd you know?"

"C'mon, son, what you told me made no sense. I could tell you were lying. I also found the dart out on the lawn."

"Wow. You're good."

"And you better be. Own up to your mistakes and learn from them and you won't have any trouble."

My mom didn't have the same level of patience with me as my dad. That was especially true when, that same year as the dart incident, I got into a fight with my sister. The rule was ironclad. Keep your hands off her even if she came at you. I tried to push her out of my room, and before I knew it, my mom had burst out of the closet, and she was like a little Mike Tyson. She threw me out of the house immediately. It was cold and pouring down rain, and I wasn't even given the opportunity to grab any of my stuff. Looking back on it, I don't blame my mom at all for what she did, but at the time I was doing a little why-me whining as I wandered the neighborhood in bare feet.

I hadn't gotten very far before Dad's pickup brake-squeaked to a stop beside me. I watched as he rolled down the window, counting the seconds until the reckoning. I knew not to lie about this one. I told him that Jasmine and I had gotten into a fight and that I'd been kicked out of the house. He nodded slowly and his head disappeared for a moment as he leaned all the way over to push the door open for me. I got back in the house then, but it was a long time before I got to get back out of the house for anything other than going to school.

You'd think I'd learned my lesson, but I snuck out of the house a few weeks later and stole a neighbor's car. Well, "stole" is kind of a strong word because the owner was this young girl who didn't mind it when we took her car out for joyrides. She'd leave the keys where we could find them, and then we'd go for a drive around the neighborhood. This time, something possessed me, and instead of just leisurely touring the nearby streets, I decided to really gun it. I was going way too fast on roads that were way too tight, and eventually ventured out of our area onto a two-lane high-way and nearly flipped it. I heard the police coming and tried to evade them. I drove the car back to the girl's house, tires squealing around the corners, and went flying up her driveway before slamming to a stop.

There, a couple of doors down, was my dad standing in the driveway. He didn't look too pleased.

Today, I know that a lot of young people, boys especially, suffer from what is now called a lack of impulse control. I didn't have a name for it back then, but I can see how that diagnosis fits. If I wanted to do something, I did it regard-less of the consequences. I don't know if enlisting in the army immediately transformed me, but I know that I started to think about my decisions with more care after going through basic. When my stress fractures kept me from moving on to airborne school immediately after basic, I think I finally started to show some sense. One of the in-structors kept encouraging me to go despite the fact that my shins were so bad. I wanted to go. I'd made some bud-dies and wanted to stick with them and I didn't want to feel like I'd somehow failed.

I resisted the temptation, and spent a few weeks putting

myself through some physical therapy. If I wasn't in the gym working on my fitness using low- to no-impact devices like the elliptical trainer, I was doing what my doctors had told me. I don't know why the RICE acronym stuck with me. Rest. Ice. Compression. Elevation. I performed each of those religiously, substituting my low-impact work for complete rest.

I did all the physical training tests and was worried about the two-mile run, but I managed to get through it basically pain-free in thirteen minutes and thirty-eight seconds. I'm glad I didn't cave in to the pressure, otherwise I would have just continued to do damage to my body, and who knows what might have happened if my shins hadn't gotten better. Airborne school, of course, meant facing my biggest fear. Even though the mock AC-130 tower was only forty feet high and you're in a harness and all, letting go and getting into that tucked-in position was one of the hardest things I'd ever had to do. I got a bad case of the shakes but I'd gotten up there by not looking down and just staring at the back of the guy in front of me.

That's a principle that I followed through most of my training. Don't think. Do as you're told. Eventually fear gives way. I was fortunate in that high winds were whipping up for the whole three weeks of airborne so we never went up on the two-hundred-fifty-foot tower, just the mock-up.

Be careful what you wish for. Not going through that next phase meant that the next time we jumped, it was going to be for real.

I'm trying to think of a word for how terrible it was. It was intense. I was a big adrenaline junkie, or at least I thought I was until that day. We got rigged up, and my parachute was good. My reserve parachute was fine. My helmet was fine. Going to the aircraft, the AC-130, I was walking out to the airfield, we were in two lines. I was in the first chalk and the second chalk was off to my right. I was walking up in the line when one of the airborne instructors, a female, pulled me off to the side. I thought I was in trouble or something. I was sitting there thinking, *What's going on?* Then I heard the words I was dreading.

"You're going to be the first one to exit."

She put me at the end of the line. I think she knew I had a fear of heights because she was with me on the tower and she saw the way I was acting. She put me at the very back of the line, the rest all filed in, and there I was, the first guy.

We got the one-minute call, the door came up, and we were already hooked up to the cable that stretched inside the length of the plane. This woman stood there, looked out, inspected everything on the outside of the aircraft, made sure there was nothing beneath us, the walkway was clear, all that good stuff. She pulled me up and handed me over to another airborne instructor, a guy. He held onto my back and he tiptoed me to the very, very edge of the aircraft.

I remember watching movies as a kid. I always thought that when you opened the door on an aircraft while it's up in the sky, you'd get sucked out. Not the case. It was extremely loud. The wind was howling. I was getting thrown around. The aircraft was shaking somewhat. And it was kind of hard to keep my balance. That's why there's a grip on the back of your parachute. The instructor was holding me there and I was partially hanging out of the aircraft and we were going maybe a hundred fifty to two hundred miles an hour. And that wind was just pushing me, pushing me, pushing me, and I was standing there with nearly every one of my muscles in spasm, and the instructors say, "Don't look down, just keep your eyes on the horizon."

I started getting weak in the knees again and I remember thinking, *What did I sign up for? This is ridiculous. I'm jumping out of an aircraft for no reason at all.*

As I stood there, from my peripheral vision I could see to my right a red light, a yellow light, and a green light. The red light was holding steady. They called thirty seconds when the yellow light came on. And that's when I thought, *Oh, my gosh. This is really happening.* The green light came on and the instructor smacked me on my ass and that's all I remember of the first few seconds. I jumped out and I remember feeling almost like getting hit by a truck, I guess, this wall of wind, just pushing me. I kept my eyes open and I was screaming out what I learned in Airborne school, counting out 1000, 2000, 3000, and on 4000 my parachute opened, I could hear the rubber bands that keep the static line held together just starting to pop.

And then I heard this boom, this push, this jolt that

slowed me down. I looked up. My blood was pumping so hard at this point. I was huffing and puffing, screaming a little bit just out of excitement. I looked up, checked my parachute, and as I was coming down I completely forgot everything I'd learned: don't look down, keep your eyes on the horizon so you don't anticipate the fall and overextend your legs and they break on landing. So, I was coming down and I could hear the wind blowing, and I was going pretty fast and landed exactly the way we weren't supposed to. I fell. I hit my feet, went straight to my ass, and tumbled on my head. I started getting dragged by my parachute. I took it off and looked up at the plane and was, like, Wow. I just jumped out of that thing.

That was an amazing feeling. Scared and excited. It was the whole mixture of feelings, just overwhelming. It was crazy. I couldn't wait to go back up and do it again as long as I was not the first guy.

That excitement didn't last long. The second jump was cool. After my third jump, I got worried about how many times a human could do this repeatedly before something bad happened. That's when the fear factor set in and I've hated jumping ever since.

I can reveal that now, but at the time I had to keep those feelings hidden from the other guys. Airborne school was interesting because you had people from all the branches, different special operations people, all there to qualify. There were a few other Ranger candidates in my chalk but we didn't really speak to each other much. We sized each other up, but even then I sensed that there was no point in being too friendly with them. First, you would most likely end up in different units, and second, this was wartime and people were getting killed. If you didn't get too close to anybody, you wouldn't hurt as much if something bad happened to them.

It's funny now to think that after Airborne, I was sent to Ranger Indoctrination Program (RIP). At the time "indoctrination" didn't mean much to me, but later I thought about how that word can mean something kind of like being brainwashed. Now it's called Ranger Assessment and Selection Program (RASP), and that's more fitting, I think. There wasn't much brainwashing going on when I went through it. It was mostly just a physical beating—long, long runs and marches of up to fifteen miles, three to four days without sleep, very little food. It's that crucible moment when you find out for yourself if you've got what it takes. My dad always used to say that the truth will out—in other words, you can't hide from who you really are and you will at some point reveal yourself.

And from the first moment you enter RIP, you're being tested. That first day I had to run a half mile carrying all my gear, a hundred pounds of it, and knowing that if I fell behind even just a bit I might be bounced out of the program. I looked like a soup sandwich at the end, but I wasn't one of the 60 or so guys out of our class of 180 who didn't make it to the end of day two. I don't know where I found the strength, but I made a promise to myself that I wasn't going to quit. If my shins flared up or my body otherwise broke down and they tossed me out, that was one thing. Quitting was not an option.

I knew that even though I was lagging behind a lot of guys in running, since my short legs weren't meant for the distance thing, I was confident that I had other skills.

The first time I fired a weapon, I was eight years old. I was down in the country with my dad and my grandfather. They did a lot of rabbit and deer hunting, and I was in a clearing with them, a bottom land and a few stands of trees. At one point, my dad handed me the gun. It felt solid but not heavy. My dad stood behind me, helped me level the gun, and then with his finger over mine, he helped me squeeze the trigger, real slow. The recoil knocked me back but my dad held me up.

I liked the sensation of firing a gun, immediately and intensely. Part of it was power, but part of it was also about control. As impulsive as I was with my homemade weapons, I was somehow able to respect what a real weapon could do and keep myself under control and eventually fire with real precision. I didn't like school, and a lot of stuff seemed really complicated to me, but what my dad taught me, sight and squeeze, seemed really simple. The simplicity of it made it fun for me. This wasn't like doing problems in math class or memorizing the Constitution's amendments, or reading a story and trying to find a theme. Sight and squeeze.

I also know that I was really angry as a kid, even until I was through with high school. I'm not really sure how firing a weapon figured into that, because I know I wasn't one of those sociopathic kids who love torturing animals. I did hunt, but I was very squeamish when it came to handling the carcasses of the rabbits and squirrels I shot. I'd ask someone else to pick them up for me. I wasn't into blood and gore, but I did get a great deal of satisfaction from mastering something. My dad would take me to the shooting range, and I developed more mental and emotional discipline there than I did anywhere else. I knew that I could never fire a weapon in anger at someone. That would mess too much with the simplicity of sight and squeeze. Sure, I felt a thrill when I was successful while hunting or hitting a target, and first going to the range, some of my anger and aggression came out. Later, precision shooting became like chess, a game that I enjoyed playing, because in order to hit a bull's-eye a lot of planning and execution had to take place.

Before I was a teenager, I had a .22 rifle with a scope and I tried to shoot a cigarette in half from a hundred yards. When I got to high school, and after spending all those hours at the range with my dad, I was able to do that regularly.

But I didn't improve just because of target practice. I also had to do some studying. When I was starting out and shooting outside, I had no clue how wind could affect a bullet's path. I figured I was only fifty to a hundred meters away from a target and a bullet traveled so fast, how could wind do anything? And the effects of gravity? Didn't even consider them.

Finally I went to the library and got a book on long-range shooting and sniping. I learned a whole lot and realized that I needed to understand better some of the math principles that I'd hated dealing with in school. I remember getting a book called *Fundamentals of Math*. It was a sixth-grade textbook, and I would sneak it home because I was in high school by that time and I knew I'd get all kinds of crap from kids at school for having it. I studied and studied that book in a way that I would never have done in a classroom. It's funny, but I was one of those kids who constantly complained that the stuff I was being forced to learn in school had nothing to do with real life. If someone had told me that math would apply to sniping, I might have paid more attention.

The more I read about sniping, the more I made the connection between chess and shooting. Anticipation, analysis, and prediction based on evidence are pretty high-level thinking skills, and I started to develop them, but if you were to ask any of my teachers if I was capable of that kind of thinking, they would have probably said no. By all outward appearances, or outside of a shooting range, I probably looked like I didn't understand the principles of cause and effect, actions and consequences.

In the army, I had to learn a lot about navigation and orienteering. It's funny to think about how I was finding my way in life as much as I was finding my way through the woods.

The Cole Range is the Rangers' version of the SEAL teams' Hell Week. That was the point at which I really learned about camaraderie and teamwork. We started out with a group of eighty or so, and by the end we were whittled down to about a dozen. The thing that kept me going was that if you decided to drop out, you had to stand there in front of everyone and say those words. I was empowered by that. Every time another guy stopped during the middle of a march or whatever and said, "I quit," I grew more determined to make it. Hearing "I quit" twenty, thirty, forty, fifty times over a four-day period can really boost your confidence when you're the one hearing it and not saying it.

I especially remember being sleep deprived and hungry as could be and being gathered near a bonfire. An instructor said, "If you just come up here, leave your team, I have a nice hot cup of coffee for you and a slice of pizza. You'll be good to go, but you've got to leave your teammates."

A few guys would go up there and take the offer, and the instructor would say, "Welcome to Korea" or "Welcome to Italy," or something similar letting the guys know that they were bound for some kind of ordinary duty. They'd sold themselves short and now they were getting the short end of the deal.

I was one of seven guys who made it through to the end. I learned that my brain might shut down or quit, but my body could keep on going, and that was a lesson that served me well throughout the rest of my career.

I was enormously proud of joining the Third Ranger Battalion in October of 2005. I was now part of the group whose legacy included the operation in Somalia that became known as Black Hawk Down, going into Grenada, fighting in the first Gulf War, rescuing Jessica Lynch. Well, not quite part of it yet. I had to report to battalion to see what my assignment was going to be.

First, Second, and Third Battalions were each doing ninety-day rotations at that point in the conflict. When I arrived at Fort Benning, I have to admit, it was a bit of a letdown. Third Battalion was in Afghanistan at the time, but I was assigned to its Charlie Company, First Platoon. That meant there wasn't a whole lot for me to do until the rest of the battalion got back. I definitely had new-kid-at-school nerves. I didn't know what to expect now that I was a Ranger, and I really wanted to make a good impression. I was there with maybe twenty other guys and they hardly even talked to me, except to issue me some equipment. I didn't have a TV or a radio, just a bed in the barracks and an iron and ironing board that I used almost constantly to press my BDUs. When I wasn't doing that, I was polishing my boots, making sure that I was as squared away as possible. I was a nineteen-year-old kid, living his dream of being an army Ranger, and I had movie visions of how my life was going to play out.

I also had a bit of a nightmare running through my mind. I'd heard that the Rangers had their own indoctrination program for the cherry new guys. I'd been told that I could expect them to come busting into my room and take me out partying or to quiz me on some bit of Ranger Battalion history or do anything to test me. When I got word, after a week of mostly just waiting, that the Third Battalion was inbound and would be down in just about an hour, I sat on the edge of my bed nearly paralyzed. When the guys came back in, I could hear them running and shouting, asking where the new guy was.

What ensued was the consumption of more beer than I'd ever seen up to that point in my young life. I'd had a few beers before, but that night was the first time I was ever drunk. I didn't want to show any kind of weakness, so I tried to keep up with them, but that wasn't really possible. A few guys asked me about myself and my background and stuff, but nothing could distract them from the drinking and the loud music and the general air of relief they all felt. They were glad to be back home, glad that they'd sustained no casualties, and clearly, I was the only one who was thinking about the fact that we had to be up at 0600 hours for formation.

I wandered away from the action and got back to my room and began laying out what I thought I had to have organized for the next day. I showed up at 0600 in my starched and pressed uniform, my dazzle-shined boots, and felt like the guy who wears a shirt and tie to the first day of school while everybody else is in jeans and T-shirts. That's mostly what the rest of the guys were wearing. I was the only one not in civilian clothes. I was escorted over to the Charlie Company CQ desk and was introduced to a very large and very forbidding looking first sergeant who I would later come to know as Black Rhino. The name fit. He was well over 220 pounds of rock-hard muscle, had a coal-black complexion, and a mouth with a missing front tooth that could make him appear either menacing or goofy.

That first time I met First Sergeant Seeley, he definitely was not goofy. He took me into a room and began his interrogation.

"Why do you want to be here? What makes you want to be a Ranger?" His voice definitely suited his body, it came out strong and deep.

I didn't know what to say, and while I was standing there, the platoon sergeant came in and stood in the doorway. I could see a little bit of light behind him, but mostly just his body filling that space.

Finally, I said, "I just want to be part of the best fighting force that the military has to offer."

The Black Rhino burst out laughing and then suddenly stopped. "No. I've heard that too many times before. I want your real answer."

I shrugged. "I just want to fight, First Sergeant. I'm here to fight and go to war."

"That's what I want to hear."

At that point, he informed me that I was going to be assigned to the Third Squad in Charlie Company as an assaulter. I was given my M4 rifle and a 203 grenade launcher. I was pretty much left on my own. There was distinct division between guys who earned their tabs—the ones who'd completed Ranger school—and the other guys like me. We were there on a trial basis, and I felt the pressure of believing that my every move was being closely monitored and evaluated. To that point, I'd not done a whole lot of specific training with weapons, and it was clear that we were being prepared for urban combat. Although I'd fired weapons before, it was a new experience to be in a small room with several other people, friendlies, knowing that you had to be very accurate.

Wearing night vision was also hard to adapt to. I don't know if my color blindness had any effect on me, but I never really liked using that device. The first time I put on PVS-14s, I got to experience what it would be like to lose an eye. The device slides down and blocks the vision in one of your eyes, and that really messes with your depth perception. I probably spent as much time bumping into things as I did making forward progress. Later, when we got into small unit training and I had to combine night vision work with my infrared laser sighting on my weapons, I had a whole new level of respect for what these guys were capable of. It was so different from open sight in daylight. Point and squeeze became my new mantra. Put the laser on the target and squeeze. Eventually, spending enough time with the night vision, figuring out what magnification settings worked for me, made me more comfortable. Our brains eventually adjust and compensate for perceiving two different images simultaneously—a near one and a far one—but it did take a lot of time.

Physical training was still rigorous with the added dimension of P-Mask runs—when you wore your protective mask, what most people think of as gas masks. We were trying to simulate the high-altitude environment of Afghanistan.

During an airport seizure drill, I really got a sense that this was now big-boy stuff. Nighttime parachuting, hotwiring vehicles to get them off the runway, lots of coordination among the various units and responsibilities.

I had never worked so hard in my life as I did in those six months prior to my first deployment. Twelve- to sixteen-hour days were the norm. Family life was nonexistent. Some of the guys told me that trying to maintain a working marriage was almost impossible, and the Ranger battalions had a really high divorce rate.

I don't know if I would have done as well as I did if it weren't for Mark Cunningham. He didn't mind me asking all kinds of questions about what it was going to be like over there—the terrain, the people, our living quarters, and anything else I could think of. I also worked the chain of command properly and wasn't afraid to ask my squad leader for clarification. I think that being the new guy and not being afraid to ask questions helped.

It was during that training cycle, during another of the many airport seizures, that I had that parachute incident when I could have easily died. I had one other near-fatal encounter, this time with a tin of Copenhagen. Mark was from Tennessee, and he said he'd been dipping tobacco since he was a pup, as he put it. One day, I was dragging, just having one of those low-energy days when I could barely keep my eyes open.

So Mark said, "If you can't stay awake, try some of this stuff." He always had a little bump below his bottom lip. He handed me the can.

I opened it and saw the dark, coarse cut of tobacco. I immediately thought of my days spent fishing and the worm dirt. I squinted at it and then at Mark.

"Here, like this." He took three fingers and pinched a bit of it.

I did as he said. At first, all I felt was a bit of warmth on the inside of my lip and then it was like someone had opened a faucet in my salivary glands. I was almost drooling, and I was trying to spit as best I could, but I could feel little bits of the tobacco going down my throat as my saliva slid down from my jaw. The next thing I knew, I was a bit dizzy and light-headed. Mark and a few other guys were laughing at me, and then suddenly my head was spinning and a moment later everything in my stomach came flying out of my mouth. The guys were laughing hysterically, and as sick as I was feeling, I couldn't really blame them.

They told me that everybody has a similar experience their first time doing dip. That was the only real hazing, if you want to call it that, I experienced. Once all the training began, we really bonded as a team. By the time we finished that intense six months and learned we were on our way to Tikrit, I thought I was really ready. Of course, I wasn't. I remember on our flight from Germany to Tikrit, I had a moment of panic when the red lights came on and the pilot announced that we were in Iraqi airspace. I thought that this was going to be like D-day. We'd land, drop the ramp, and run off with bullets flying all around us. That's when the panic set in. I didn't have any magazines of ammo with me or in my weapon. I tried to calm myself by saying that I could borrow some from one of the other guys. How could I have been so stupid as to not load my weapon.

When we landed, the ramp did go down, but we didn't take any enemy fire. We all loaded into vans, kind of like airport hotel vans, and as we drove off, I saw the familiar arches of a McDonald's, a Burger King, and what was unfamiliar, a Green Bean coffee store.

Nothing could have prepared me for the smell though.

Diesel fuel and oil, human excrement. Still, the first time I set foot on Iraqi soil, I felt a thrill of pleasure. Wow. I'm here. I'm in combat.

I was still a bit out of it from the Ambien, the long hours of sleep, and the sense of disorientation that comes from climbing into an aircraft in one part of the world and climbing off it in another. We were told that we'd be conducting an operation that night. The briefing was a blur, and then what seemed like minutes later, we did a final check before mounting up. My squad leader came up to me and said, "Everything good to go? Give me a heads-up."

"Batteries good, roger that."

He rechecked my lasers, my night vision, my radio, both of us checking and rechecking everything.

Cunningham approached me and nodded. "Don't worry about it. Everything's going to be good to go. Should be in and out."

Next thing I knew I was sitting in the doorway of a Black Hawk helicopter, squeezed between two other squad members, the pilot making sharp turns while flares and the rounds from the miniguns lit up the sky. I was startled by the sound of what seemed to be a chain saw, but it was just the laser array emitting more tracers downrange. When we got to the one-minute mark, I leaned out against my straps and saw this lone building in the middle of all this flatness.

Oh, crap, this is it.

As soon as that thought was complete, the helicopter flared to scrub off all its speed. Like a horse being brought to a sudden halt, the helicopter rose nose first and its ass end settled, and we were in a near hover.

Stepping onto the ground, I thought of the moon. The soil where we'd landed was so fine and dustlike that it reminded me of the images I'd seen as a kid of our astronauts jumping around on the moon, kicking up little dust clouds. I didn't have time to get lost in space. Everyone around me was moving, seemingly in different directions, guys zigzagging, cutting off angles to the building. I remembered that my team was responsible for covering and cutting off anybody coming out of the right side of the building. I was really shocked by how fast everything was happening. By the time I was able to make sense of what I was seeing, half the team was already making entry into the door of the building. I was still fifty meters away. I noticed the quiet, the absence of the sound of helicopters.

I finally got my stuff together and ran toward the angle I was supposed to cover. As I was moving, I heard a loud pop. At first it didn't register, but then I realized it was the flash grenades/bangers going off. I tried to picture what was taking place inside the building, but more than that, I was wishing I was inside there. I'd been told that nothing we did in training could really prepare you for the real thing. It was kind of like the difference between a practice and an actual game. Yes, you were told that you should practice with the same intensity you'd bring to the game, but the violence of action they'd talked about didn't really compare.

What bothered me as I sat loading my weapon before we left was realizing that I might have to fire these live rounds at another human being. You couldn't really train for that reality. I grew up in a religious family, and obviously, "thou shall not kill" is something we all believed in and put into practice. As I was sitting there on the Black Hawk, all kinds of thoughts were flying around in my head. By the time we'd reached the objective, I was really numb to all those thoughts and feelings and just kind of went on autopilot. That's what all that training was for—just do the things you'd done dozens of times before, don't think too much, just respond.

The mission went well. We killed two of the targets and apprehended a third. What I remember most is getting back to base and eating chow and watching CNN. Our mission was a breaking-news headline. I thought of all those people in all those airport terminals waiting for their flights half listening to what was going on in my part of the world.

I'd arrived.

Me with an SPR (5.56 77gr.) in Jalalabad Afghanistan as
the platoon's designated marksman. 2007

Jalalabad Afghanistan squad-designated marksman. 2007

Me with Pemberton brushing up on our high-angle long-range shooting. 2008

Back after an overwatch and surveillance position during a platoon exercise. 2008

Practicing long-range shooting, standing with the .300 Win Mag. 2008

After an intense firefight and night raid in Afghanistan Helmand province. 2009

We had just got word we were working with RECCE. Pemberton and I working on spotter/sniper drills with my SR-25. 2009

Pemberton and me overwatching the Marines as they began entry into the village. 2009

Watching a Taliban target more than 700 yards away and prepping to take the shot. 2009

Pemberton on the roof with me overwatching the Marines.
We had been without sleep for days at this point. 2009

After taking out the Taliban target and making sure the Marines exfil was successful, Pemberton (REECE) and me. It was a worthy picture moment. 2009

Me with the RECCE communications member after the long-shot and all-night sniper hide. 2009

The terrain we were pinned down in against the Chechen sniper. 2009

Pemberton and me soaked in blood and water coming through the door with Cpl. Benjamin Kopp being carried out behind us. We had already been fighting for more than four hours continuously. 2009

Cpl. Benjamin Kopp being carried, by his machine gun that saved us from the Chechen just minutes before. 2009

On the roof providing sniper fire on targets as we call in a MEDEVAC for the wounded. 2009

The large blue doors of the compound leading out to the Marines,
preparing to run through hostile open terrain. 2009

Cpl. Benjamin Kopp.

After a successful all-night firefight and special
operations raid on an HVT in Helmand. 2009

Me with the Barrett .50 cal sniper rifle in Afghanistan. 2009

Our last photo as a platoon on the
airfield in Kandahar. 2009

Sgt. Anibal Santiago. The father figure of the sniper section.

Presented to

SGT NICHOLAS IRVING

You know what you are . . . what you're made of. War is in your blood. Don't fight it. You didn't kill for your country. You killed for yourself. God's never gonna make that go away. When you're pushed, killing's as easy as breathing.

John J. Rambo

5 NOVEMBER 2008 - 9 MARCH 2010

From the men of 3RD Ranger Battalion Sniper Section for exemplary service and heroism.

RANGERS LEAD THE WAY

The quote on my sniper section plaque.

Contracting near the southern Texas border. 2011

Two weeks after my deployment, I immediately entered the International Sniper Competition at Ft. Benning, Georgia, placing top five.

Observing an Afghan village with Pemberton during our five-day recon.

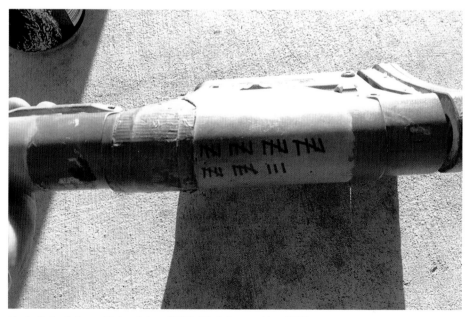

My buttstock from Afghanistan, 2009. 33 ticks marking EKIA.

5. A Long Day of Reckoning

By the time I'd gotten to Afghanistan and my deployment as a sniper team leader with Pemberton and the rest of the guys, I'd become used to the idea that we were making headlines. At that point those stories weren't major ones and I knew that back home a lot of people had grown tired of our involvement in Afghanistan. It had to seem to them that nothing was ever going to change. We didn't take that attitude at all. I was beginning to see that the Taliban really had their boots on the neck of many of the civilians, that the people were caught up in a big mess not of their own making. Regardless, we had a job to do and a way to put our training to its best use.

Even though we'd had those two days off, I think everybody could sense that this was not going to be a typical deployment. The high operational tempo of those first few days had really set the tone. You could tell that morale was high because of what was going on. Some of the guys in the squad were so hyped up they couldn't sleep well, so all-night movie marathons went on, and eventually some of the guys were in the computer room watching replays of our missions, looking at the satellite feeds, anticipating what our next objectives might be, and doing their own form of recon. I think that, to a man, we sensed that there'd be another mission coming up and that kept us at a high pitch.

Our forty-man platoon was housed in its own separate area, so we didn't have much contact with anyone else, but even within that small group, Pemberton and I were the only snipers. It wasn't like there was a rule that you only hung out with the guys who did the same job or were in your squad, but most of the other Rangers we were with had deployed together. Because you carried out the same role with the same guys, you naturally spent more time with them and got to know them better. To put it in football terms, it was as if you had the offense and the defense, and Pemberton and I were the kicker and the punter. Other guys from those first two units also worked with us as part of the overall special teams unit, but there was only one of him and only one of me. I was back, in a sense, to being that new kid at school.

Pemberton and I had been through training together and we were pretty tight, but we both knew that sitting around together on our off hours was a recipe for disaster. During training we had been with other spotters and snipers who'd been paired off, and in some ways we were like married couples. And if you hang around with enough married people, you probably know someone like Thomas and Albright. After we discovered how much the two of them got into verbal fights with each other, we referred to them as Itchy and Scratchy, after the TV cartoon characters on *The Simpsons*. They shared a room, and they were almost like little kids, brothers, who argued over who got to sleep on which level of the bunk beds.

The walls of our rooms were just sheets of metal, so they weren't exactly soundproof. The rest of us would be in our room lying in bed and we'd hear Itchy and Scratchy going after each other.

"You suck."

"No. You suck."

"You suck worse. Why can't you give me the right windage?"

"What? You suck at windage. Don't complain to me about that."

"Yeah. Well, you suck worse."

"No. You suck."

It wasn't exactly a battle of wits, but still we would laugh and laugh and egg them on.

Next morning, we'd see the two of them at chow eating breakfast, and you could never have guessed that they were pissed at each other the night before. People aren't consistent, but I was surprised that if you started to say something bad about Itchy to Scratchy, he wouldn't come to his buddy's defense; he'd agree with you and add something to top your negative remark.

Pemberton and I never got into those kinds of fights. We could disagree with each other, but it wasn't a constant thing, and we didn't provide all kinds of entertainment for the rest of the guys. Maybe that was because we made a conscious effort to get out and get to know the rest of the guys in first platoon. I may have a bit of ADD because I sometimes get bored really easy, and getting to know the other guys was a way to avoid having things get stale in my marriage to Pemberton. Those first couple of days off were our opportunity to start developing bonds with the other guys, and while I can't say we became a family over the course of those first couple of nights, we did make a start at it.

Our fifth day in, Pemberton and I were out on a little ledge, what we called "the balcony," of our building, cleaning our weapons, sitting there in shorts and T-shirts. He was telling me about a cousin of his who was big-time into motorcycles and was planning a round-the-world trip on his bike. Some of the snipers from second platoon came over and wanted to talk shop with us. They were pretty open about being envious of us. They hadn't seen any real action to that point, so they were into talking about tactics. Were we doing holdovers, dialing in our scopes on guys? It was all still pretty new to us, so we were happy to swap stories.

As we were talking, I spotted a couple of guys with long beards and dirt-covered faces and clothes. It was almost like I'd spotted Bigfoot or something. We all knew that these guys existed, but you seldom saw one out and about. I recognized one of them because we'd been in battalion together, and what we called the RECCE guys (Regimental Reconnaissance Division—a special unit within the Rangers) were legendary. This was my first actual sighting of any on that deployment. As much as I thought it was cool to be a sniper, and as much as some guys thought my job was the best, I admired the RECCE guys and what they got to do. I liked the stalking part of my sniper training, building hides and camouflaging myself and all that, and I'd never really gotten to use those skills in actual combat. (That is, I really liked it if I knew there were no spiders involved.) Call me a kid, but who wouldn't like going around playing a very complicated and very high-stakes game of hide-and-seek? Those guys were gone for days and sometimes weeks living outside the wire in tents and really roughing it. They looked so scraggly partly because it helped them blend into the environment and partly because hygiene wasn't a big priority given their task.

Davis came up to me and said, "Hey, man. We've got to talk."

Given my inglorious past, I immediately thought, *What did I do wrong?*

What I said was, "Sure. What's going on?"

He led me away from the rest of the group. "Been hearing good things about you. We've been tracking this target for quite some time. We can get eyes on him but that's it."

I looked over his shoulder and saw all the snipers from the other platoons staring at us.

"He's been within a thousand maybe. Can you make that? If he's at that range and in a car moving, can you make the shot?"

I took a deep breath. I didn't want to make any promises I couldn't keep, and I also didn't want to disappoint him. "That's a really long shot for my weapon. If I had a Win Mag that would be one thing, but with the .308, not likely. With the Win Mag, yes, but only if the vehicle was coming at me head-on."

"Got it. We can make it happen."

He filled me in on the rest of the details. They just wanted me and Pemberton and a few other select guys. They were two weeks away from going back home, and they wanted to wrap up this deployment in a neat little package by neutralizing this one very important target.

"So, like this is a pretty secretive thing, right?"

Davis shrugged. "Somewhat."

I was pretty excited, to put it mildly. I stood there thinking. A week behind enemy lines? Fully self-supporting with our own food, water, and ammo? Tracking this single target. I was jumping up and down on the inside. *Hell, yeah!*

"Well, yeah, sure. We could tag along," I said.

Later, I relayed the information I'd received to Pemberton, and Caleb and Julian, two other snipers. Pemberton's eyes lit up and he set down his cleaning supplies and dashed out of the room. He came back with a rucksack and started stuffing it with everything he could find.

"Whoa, dude. Calm down," I told him. "We don't have any intel yet. We don't even have confirmation the plan's a go."

"I don't care. I dream about doing this stuff."

I had to agree. To that point, we hadn't heard of any of our snipers doing this kind of operation in Afghanistan—extended time behind enemy lines, stalking and tracking.

Caleb and Julian were pissed.

"Why you two? Why do we get stuck with the regular operations?"

I felt bad for them, well, not too bad, and said, "I don't make the rules. We got lucky and got into a lot of action right away, a bunch of kills. They want to go with the hot hands, I guess."

"Roger that. Makes sense, but still."

I couldn't really sleep after hearing about this possibility, so I went to the TOC, the Tactical Operations Center, and on my way, I saw four of the RECCE guys, including Davis, outside their tent.

I couldn't contain my excitement. I went over to them and said, "Hey, listen, I'm going down to the TOC. If you guys want to go with me, we can look at a few maps and get a better sense of what you guys want to do. As a sniper, I like to get a good feel for the environment and especially the terrain. The colors, you know. Have to bring the ghillie suit and need to camouflage our equipment. It is good to get a sense of the buildings, in case my range finder craps out, the batteries go—"

I realized I was rambling, but it was enthusiastic rambling and the RECCE guys agreed to join me. We spent the next few hours viewing maps and going over other intel they provided. Pemberton joined us, and I was really, really feeling good about things. This was what I'd joined the army to do, and now I was doing it. I was also impressed by one of the guys in the TOC. He wore a backpack with some kind of satellite receiver in it, and he had an earpiece through which he could listen to all different transmissions from the eyes in the sky to guys on the ground. He was helping us track this target's movement and it was like we were getting updates in real time. I was so fired up, I decided not to wait to go to our platoon sergeant to fill him in and to get his permission to pursue this opportunity.

He was out of it that night, and I must have banged on his door for five minutes before he finally woke up. I started filling him in on what the plan was, going into a lot of detail. He listened patiently and then said, "Cool. No problem. Do what you have to do. We'll get a couple of other snipers to go with us for the next few days." I needed to let

Sergeant Casey know what we were doing so he could grab the remaining two snipers from second platoon. It kind of sucked for them because they would then have to run ops for both their unit and mine.

Later the next morning, I reported to the commander and he was also very supportive. He just wanted to make sure that we were going to be safe and that our plan was a good one. We also had come up with a plan B, which he was glad to hear about, as well as backups for us in case things went sideways. He knew that we were a valuable asset, and having eliminated as many bad guys as we had to that point worked in our favor.

Pemberton and I spent the next three days packing and we kept debating the different priorities. We had to balance going light and suffering if we didn't have the proper amount of food and clothing and water. We each ended up carrying eighty pounds of gear after experimenting with different proportions. I must have put my rucksack on the scale twenty times each day. The two of us were busy little dudes while everyone else in our platoon was taking it easy, walking around and calling home. We tried to keep a low profile, but when you're packing your gear and stacking ammo all around, guys are going to be curious. We couldn't tell them what we were up to, and that didn't sit well with some of the guys. Just saying that we were going out with the RECCE guys fed into their desire to know. Fact is, even if I could have told them who we were going after, I wouldn't have been able to. I didn't even know the target's name at that point.

Once the green button was pushed, Pemberton and I made our way over to our new teammates' tent. My jaw dropped when I saw how many large bags these guys were going to bring along. They had portable satellite dishes and what looked like enough batteries to stock a Radio Shack store. I also noticed that they had native clothing, a *kameez,* a long dresslike robe, and a *pakol,* or rounded hat, that sat on top of long hair they'd dyed to better blend in with the locals. A lot of times the RECCE guys had to move among the population undetected. I thought that was kind of cool, going undercover, but it was something I didn't think I'd be able to pull off myself. I was glad that I had one job. Take this target out.

The final version of the plan called for us to be out in the field tracking this guy. Once we had eyes on him, we'd call in a platoon to help support us. Whether it was going to be the guys in first platoon that Pemberton and I were with wasn't clear. It was going to be a case of calling in whoever was closest to our location. I felt good about the plan, especially knowing that we had thirty-five to forty other Rangers who were going to be called in.

I was used to flying in Chinooks, but it was weird to just have six guys in a compartment as big as the ones Chinooks had. Usually you're crammed in there, but all that empty space was a reminder that for the first part of this operation, tracking the target, we were on our own. Of course, we were going to be in constant communication with command, but still. Even the crew chiefs were a little surprised to see us. As we loaded onto the ramp with hundreds of pounds of gear, sniper rifles, and bearded men, one of them looked at us and asked, "Who are you guys? Delta, Rangers, SEALs?"

Derek, another of the RECCE group and their leader, looked at him and yelled over the sound of the turbines and rotors, "We're just regular guys."

The crew chief shook his head, knowing that he was being lied to and knowing that asking again wouldn't do any good.

Things got a little worse just before takeoff.

Derek told us, "We've got a twenty-five-mile hike ahead of us as soon as we hit the ground. Get some sleep."

I started shaking my head, and I know my eyes were wide as saucers.

From behind Derek's beard I could see his teeth. "No, man. We're meeting up with some marines. Stay with them for a bit, and operate out of their little camp."

He went back to sit down and a minute later we were airborne. I heard the pilot swearing up and down as we took on mortar fire. He made evasive maneuvers and then climbed as rapidly as he could, getting us above the max ordinance where they thought the projectile could reach. Once I could feel that we'd leveled off, I unclipped my safety line and tried to get some sleep. I shut my eyes and reviewed the maps in my mind. When we got the one-minute out call, I staggered up to one knee, struggling with all that gear I had in my ruck. I took one more look at the terrain below us. I couldn't see any structures at all, and I wondered how those marines could be out there in the middle of nowhere.

As we were offloading, a marine came up to Davis and asked him who we were. Before he could respond, the marine said, "Don't tell me. Delta Company. SEAL team 6, right?"

The guy knew the drill; special ops guys couldn't tell anybody else who they were. Shrugging into my pack, I looked out across the way and all I could see was one small building that looked like it was surrounded by impact holes from mortar rounds, about six feet in circumference. Out of the rotor wash, one marine emerged from the dust cloud wearing nothing but a T-shirt and underwear. He had a lit cigar clamped between his teeth.

"Hey, guys, welcome to our little home. Just follow me. We're going to get you guys situated."

As we made our way toward the building, I noticed that in each of those holes, someone was sleeping. I saw them there, and I thought I'd never again complain about the air-conditioning being too cold or not cold enough or the chow not being as hot as it should be. These guys had it rough.

After the marine in charge led us into the building, we all stood there looking around at nothing much.

He gestured around the single room with its bare floor and four walls.

"This is the spot, guys. You can do whatever you want in here. I know you are going to be in and out all the time. Don't worry about my guys asking you any questions, they get the drill. Just do what you have to do and good luck."

With that, he left us, leaving behind a trail of cigar smoke.

The RECCE group began to immediately set up the comm links and satellite equipment, making calls and consulting their laptop. I heard them checking in to let the commanders know that we'd landed and passing along our coordinates. I immediately grabbed my 550 cord—a rope that could support that much weight—and started stringing up a hammock-type sleeping spot. Calling it a "sleeping spot" isn't very accurate. Torture rack would be better. Even though I'd brought hundreds of feet of the stuff, there still wasn't enough to make a really solid surface. I remember my mom buying a beef roast that was all trussed up with string, and when she cut that away, there were all these indentations in the meat. Well, that was what was happening to my body, and that meant my circulation was being cut off.

I don't know if I would have slept much even on a decent

bunk. I was wrapped up in paying attention to the comm device. I wanted to keep track of what was going on back with our guys in the first. There was a whole lot of static and fits and bursts of sound and flashes on the display. I kept seeing TIC come across the screen and my heart raced. TIC stood for "troops in contact." That meant that our guys were either taking fire, firing on the opposition, or in most cases, exchanging fire with the enemy.

All I could think of was that I was out there in the middle of a hot Afghan summer, tired, hungry, and sore, and those guys were getting into some really cool action. For the first three days, we'd gone out on a couple of patrols, going to locations based on what the RECCE guys had seen on their laptop. The recon stuff didn't last all day, and I spent most of my time messing with my gear and hearing and seeing TIC coming in. Those guys back there must have gotten into a bunch of stuff, because at least ten to fifteen times those three little letters kept teasing me.

I was concerned about the differences in terrain we might have to operate in, so I was spray painting my weapon, my clothes, in an attempt to do a better job of blending in. Finally, after four days, we got orders that the third platoon was going to work in support of us. We were to mount up in a truck and travel to another Marine base where our Ranger buddies would be. As we were rolling along in the truck, I noticed all these red markers sticking up out of the ground on both sides of our path of travel. I asked the driver what they were.

He looked startled and said, "That's where the land mines are. This whole area is mined. Leftovers from when the Afghans and the Soviets were going at it. We can't veer left or right, otherwise we'd be right in the middle of them."

"You kidding me?"

"Hell, no."

"So, if we start taking hits, I can't even get out of this rig and lay down effective fire?"

"That's right. Unless you want to get your ass blown up. I'm going to just keep on driving and get us out of here."

I looked around me. All we had for protection was the canvas top. It was a long twenty-five minutes until we arrived at the base, a small mud-and-concrete Afghan school. A large group of marines had also just arrived and they gave us a hand unloading.

I said to Pemberton, "I've got some of my own unloading to do."

"Yeah."

"Finally," I said. "Three days is a long time. Maybe that truck ride shook it loose. MREs." Pemberton laughed, knowing that between us those letters didn't stand for "meals ready to eat" but "meals refusing to exit."

I got to experience my own *Platoon* moment, relieving myself in a cardboard box the size of a phone booth, pouring gas on it, and then watching later as a marine rolled out a barrel of our collective waste and set fire to it. Guys were walking around shirtless and sweating, and even though there weren't any palm trees around, I could have sworn I was in Vietnam someplace. Only we weren't going to be greeted by the smell of napalm in the morning, we were going to come under serious fire from the Taliban. The marines filled us in, letting us know that every morning at around five, just before sunup, we'd come under attack. The same thing had been happening day after day regular as clockwork.

I found Pemberton and let him know my plan. We'd set up a hide site and when those bad guys came in to fire on the school, we'd take them out.

"I'm in."

Not only was Pemberton in, but the Marine captain was as well. That was after he became comfortable with the idea that it wasn't going to be an entire platoon of Rangers, just me and Pemberton. At first he said, "You're just going to go into an established village with known Taliban members and kill them just to help us out?"

"That's the plan."

In the end, we figured it was best to take a RECCE guy with us to keep comms in place and to notify chain of command what was going on, both back at the Marine base and with our Ranger platoon.

It had been ninety-six hours since I'd gotten anything

near decent sleep, and I'm sure that contributed to the sur-real impressions that night left me with. The sun was an-gling lower and Pemberton and I put on our ghillie suits and headed out along with McDonald to set up that hide site. In the low light, night vision wasn't as effective as it could have been, and I found myself staggering a bit. I led the formation out of the back of the Marine compound, and I immediately picked up a scent. With the wind at my back, Pemberton and McDonald were leaving a scent trail as strong as anything I'd ever smelled. I knew that I was no spring breeze myself, and in that case that was a good thing. Blending in with your surroundings meant doing so in every way possible. Fresh soap smell or a clean body was a sure giveaway.

We crept along, going about as slowly as I ever had on any march, and the quiet was almost overwhelming. Know-ing that there are other armed personnel out there who are bent on getting at you is a weird feeling, especially at night. It's like your thoughts expand to fill up all the darkness, the blank black chalkboard ahead of you. I spotted a small outbuilding at one point, and thought it offered a good view of a wide-open field anyone coming toward the ma-rines' position would have to cross. We'd have plenty of time to put eyes on them and communicate with the ma-rines. I wanted McDonald to enter the building first. He had an M4 assault carbine and it was the best weapon to use in that confined space. He also had a thirty-round magazine and a suppressor, all tactically superior for that application than my twenty rounds and my 308. Pemberton was behind us with his monster Win Mag, and I knew that if it came to him having to fire off rounds in that building, we were maybe beyond worst-case scenario and into some serious, serious trouble.

Using hand signals and moving far more slowly than we would have during a normal clearing operation, we determined that nobody was home. I was relieved to be able to stretch my muscles a bit. All that superslow-motion stuff had me cramping a bit. I gulped down nearly a full CamelBak of water. I figured it was about 0330 hours and we had until just before dawn before we'd see any activity at all. It wasn't going to take us long to set up the hide, considering that the building was only about twenty by twenty in size and windowless. Three guys. No windows. Not much real thinking to be done. We fashioned a hide on the roof.

How to get through the next eight hours was going to occupy my mind entirely. Just before we came on this RECCE operation, I'd bought a pack of cigarettes from an Afghan market. They were foul-tasting things, like inhaling the smoke from a soggy campfire, but in the first hour or so, I managed to go through the entire pack. I felt like I'd swallowed a stick and it was lodged in my chest cavity, my mouth was coated with a foul-tasting soot that I couldn't spit clear, and I was wired. All that nicotine was doing a horse race through my bloodstream, and I could have sworn I could see hoofs and clods of dirt being kicked up in the throbbing veins of my wrist. I could hardly keep still, and with my legs bouncing and my eyes twitching, I sat as the minutes crept by. I played little games with myself, trying to count to sixty in the exact amount of time it would take for the second hand on my watch to complete a revolution. I'd wait for the little line to get to the twelve, look away while counting and then take a quick glance once I got to sixty to see how I'd done. After a while, I turned that into a kind of competition, with me squaring off against my imaginary friend Dave, keeping track of how many seconds we were both off, totaling them after five rounds.

Somehow, I got to the time when the first bit of yellow and reddish light bled across the horizon. Pemberton had dozed off for a while, and McDonald was on the comms. At one point, he patched me in to the marines' commander. He let me know that they'd decided to not sit and wait for the attack. They were going to assume a position roughly halfway between the village and their compound. That was going to put them about a quarter mile from our location, out of the range of our fire. I agreed that was a good plan, and he shared with us their route and ETA. We'd be able to provide cover fire for them if necessary.

No more than twenty minutes or so later, we had them in our sights. I was following them through my scope, when I heard at first one, and then a moment later, a series of snaps. They were lighting up a nearby compound on the edge of the village. I heard a few louder concussive booms and knew that they were firing RPGs, except we could hear them going over our heads and back toward the marines' compound. The Taliban were retaliating. Over the comms came a report a few seconds later that they'd taken a hit and a marine was KIA. In our sleep-deprived state, Pemberton and I scrambled around on the roof. Once up there I realized we'd both left our helmets with McDonald. That much weight on your head while looking through a scope for an extended period of time was way too taxing. We didn't have time to do much about that.

I was pissed at that point. I observed the area hoping that someone would enter my crosshairs. I knew I had to make sure that we didn't fire on any friendlies, but I was starting to feel like if I didn't do something assertive and soon, I was going to lose it. I calmed myself by sighting on as much as I could. A small firefight was going on at that point, but all I could see was our marines and their position. Eventually, as I panned side to side, I saw something glint in the early morning sunlight. Silhouetted against the eastern sky was a single figure on a moped. I couldn't see what was attached to the back of his vehicle, but it looked like little flagpoles or something. I couldn't be sure if he was a Taliban dude or some local who was going to work somewhere and had his tools strapped to his moped.

I knew I needed to keep an eye on him. He dismounted

his moped and he unstrapped a sack that was cinched to a rack behind the seat. He slung the sack over his shoulder and walked behind a building. I sighted on him, on the building, on his moped, took a dimension on him from his groin to the top of his head. Since the locals were generally shorter than American men, I estimated the dimensions to be around 35 inches instead of 40. I employed a rule of thumb. In my scope, he measured approximately 1.2 mils or 740 meters away.

"Pemberton, you got the guy on the moped at ten o'clock. Track him with me and follow up in case."

"Roger that."

I stared at that lone figure for a few more minutes, watching his movements. For a second or two, he went out of my scope as he hunched down. When he stood again, I could see that what I thought were the handles of shovels or other tools were RPGs. He raised the weapon to his shoulder and leaned far out from behind the building he was tucked behind. I could see a Marine Humvee about fifty meters from his position, on maybe a ten-degree angle from where he was at, essentially a straight-on shot. In my head, I could see everything playing out—the rocket impacting the vehicle, the five guys inside being ejected from the flaming wreck.

I sighted again and determined that the attacker was still approximately 740 meters away. I knew I didn't have a whole lot of time, so I couldn't pick out a specific location on his body. I squeezed the trigger and watched the bullet drop into his body. I was hoping to make contact, do something to keep him from firing that RPG. It felt to me like it took forever for that bullet to impact him, but it did and he went down in a heap, with his face between his legs. This was the farthest shot for me to date. Watching the bullet's vapor trail travel to the target had me feeling serene. It took only less than a second before that .308 married itself to his body, but it felt like a lifetime. Some of his guys noticed what had happened and dragged his body and the weapon back behind the building.

Pemberton and I started to pepper that building and I watched as he took out another guy who foolishly stood up and fired his AK. The round got him in the hip area and spun him. He lay there twisted and twitching for a few seconds, still firing rounds haphazardly before he stilled. The marines had moved back for a bit, but after Pemberton's kill, they advanced. Bullets were still snapping by all around us, but now they were getting closer. The Taliban fighters must have figured out that we were up on that roof and they started hammering the building.

I started to freak out thinking I was going to get snapped in the head since I was helmetless. McDonald was down below us, still on comms, and with all the gunfire going on, he couldn't hear us. I low-crawled over the ledge near a small window and leaned over and started shouting, "Helmets! Helmets! Helmets!" as loud as I could. Suddenly two helmets came flying up in the air, whizzing past my head. If one of them had hit me, I would have been knocked unconscious. McDonald's throws were excellent. The helmets clattered onto the roof and sat there spinning slowly. Pemberton and I grabbed them and strapped them on, both of us knowing we should have never put ourselves in that position.

We resumed laying down suppressive fire. McDonald joined us at that point, unloading that M4. Bullets were impacting all around us. I could see little dirt devils being kicked up near my feet and legs, but I just kept firing. Finally, after about five minutes of the marines firing and us firing, the Taliban fled, retrieving their dead and retreating to their position within the village.

The quiet was unnerving, broken only by the sound of voices coming over the comms. We were informed that the second platoon had arrived; Pemberton and I were to rejoin the rest of the RECCE team and resume our intended mission. As we made our way back toward the Marine compound to meet up with the rest of our team, a few of the marines approached us, thanking us for our help. They were glad that I'd taken out the RPG dude especially. Their top gunner had spotted him, but in trying to get a bead on him, the .50 cal had jammed.

We talked for a while longer, and then our guys from the second showed up. Cody, a little guy from the Bronx, came up to me and pushed me in the chest, smiling and saying,

"The Reaper. We knew it was you, man. As soon as we landed, we could hear a firefight going on to our right in the distance. We heard that single shot crack off. Knew it had to be you. The Reaper."

"What are you talking about with this Reaper stuff?"

Treadwell joined us and said, "You haven't heard? There's some wild shit being talked about you killing, like, seven hundred guys, so they call you the Reaper now."

I shook my head. I liked the name, but the stories were out of control. "Are you kidding me?"

"No, man. You know how these things go."

I knew it was useless to try to stop guys from talking. The Ranger community was kind of like a big school class. Somebody did something and by the time the story had spread, it went from a guy having drunk a six-pack to him knocking over a liquor store and delivering twenty kegs to a party along with a few dozen sorority girls from the local college.

We stayed at the Marine compound for a few hours. We did a quick briefing, but we'd been at it for four days now, and we all knew what the plan was. I liked the idea of us being able to freelance a bit to help out the marines. I was feeling good about what we'd done, but knowing that somebody had lost their life took a lot of the gratification out of it. We were sitting around with a few of the marines playing cards and talking. One of them, a black guy named Samuels, was talking about the man who was KIA.

"Good guy. Helluva soldier. Just the worst stinking feet ever though." He laid down his cards. "Fold."

"Sorry about what happened."

Samuels stretched and then rotated his head around to loosen up his neck muscles, "No worries. It happens. Guys get killed out here. It's war."

A few of the other marines chimed in, echoing what Samuels said.

I knew that I couldn't dwell on it for too long. If I wanted to make sense of that marine's death, the one way I could do it was by taking out that Taliban HVT we'd been tracking. An eye for an eye was about the best you could do.

We switched it up and I played a few hands of Texas hold 'em, but the cards being laid down began to swim in my vision. I knew I needed some sleep. I stepped away from the guys and lay down in the dirt. I found a round, smooth stone and used it as a pillow. I was lying on my back and I could feel my stomach bile rising into my throat. I heard a strange whistling sound, high-pitched and persistent, and wondered if we were going to come under attack again. It didn't matter. The next thing I knew I woke up and the last of the day's shadows were retreating. Pretty soon we would be after it again. I was hoping that things would go according to plan. As we climbed into the deuce and half and rolled on, I knew that the original plan had changed. Instead of it just being me and Pemberton and the other RECCE guys, we were joined by the entire second platoon, four truckloads' worth of men and equipment. It was good to have them as backup and support, but I wondered how this was going to play out now that we weren't moving fast and light. Was somebody not telling me something?

6. The Chechen Comes Calling

You never know how stress and sleeplessness are going to affect you. As we rolled along in the trucks, I was struck by just how beautiful the area was. The moon was up and full, and we'd entered a desert area with rolling dunes. Beauty can also be a beast, or at least it can turn your beasts of burden into two and a half tons of lawn ornaments. The sand wasn't too deep, the dunes were more like waves of sand, but some of the trucks bogged down. Eventually, it didn't make much sense for us to try to get any farther on four wheels. We exited the trucks and formed up. So much for all the preplanning and scouting we'd done. Our target had moved on into an extremely remote and desolate area. Flying in would have revealed our position and intentions, the trucks couldn't get through, so we were left to our own two feet.

I wasn't looking forward to the march. I was already exhausted, had catalogued the memories of the assist we gave to the marines in a mental file called "the Longest Day," and I knew that it was only going to get longer. Yet, when I looked out across the moonlit desert landscape, I thought, *This looks like a scene from* Aladdin. *I wish that Pemberton and I could just ride a magic carpet to our objective.*

The thought and the image were so ridiculous to me that I started to laugh. Pemberton looked at me with a puzzled expression. I managed to stifle my giggle and said, "I can't even tell you right now what's going on in my head."

"I hear you. I'm so friggin' tired."

I heard him, but I was still picturing the two of us sitting on that carpet, cruising above the landscape, some corny-ass Disney tune playing in the background.

Five hours later, all I was thinking was that this just sucked. We'd been marching for hours, and it was like we'd been walking in boot-sucking mud the entire time. Those little dunes, the ones that seemed like the ripples on a potato chip, were exhausting. Every step we had to lift one foot up, trying to maintain our balance, and then push off and go, all the while fighting our way through one another's divots. It was a hamstring-and-quadriceps-killing exercise in stop-motion agony. Worse, the sun was coming up, and that meant that we'd be doing the operation in full-on daytime, having our position exposed in the sunlight.

Every now and then the terrain would change, rocky soil and a few stream crossings, the water just high enough to get over your boots, and the rocks slick enough and the current powerful enough to knock you off balance. Maintaining noise discipline was tough, especially with that many guys, and in that high desert valley, it seemed as if sounds could travel miles uninterrupted. We couldn't talk to each other, obviously, but every time one of us staggered or slipped, we'd involuntarily make some noise, have our gear rattle a little bit. Being stuck inside your own head after that many hours, and being so exhausted and sleep-deprived, you were in a place you didn't want to be mentally. Random weirdness rattled around in there. I took to singing a little song in my mind to keep those other thoughts at bay. In time with my footfalls, I was chanting, "This—sucks. This—sucks," on and on.

Finally, we got within a half mile of the objective. That's when the RECCE team and Pemberton and I split off. We made our way about eight hundred meters from the main element. I was on point and discovered a large hole, maybe two meters wide and a meter deep. I pointed it out to Pemberton and he nodded. We wanted to mentally mark that location in case we needed it if things got bad. We kept going and then stopped and took our position in a large open field, now some thousand meters from the rest of the platoon. We were responsible for making sure that no one fled the area. The plan had been to check in with the main unit once we'd established ourselves.

I tried my radio. I got nothing in return. Pemberton tried his. Same thing. McDonald tried his. Three for three. We're lying in the middle of this open field and we've got shaky communications at best. Radio malfunctions and radio weirdness plagued us all the time, in a nerve-jangling version of Murphy's Law.

At one point, two men on a bike came up on our position. I had to stop them. I aimed my mounted PEQ-15's visible laser right on the chest of the guy riding on the handlebars, hoping he'd notice that dot. He did. The bike came to a stop. We were pretty well camouflaged, so I rose up just a bit and signaled to them, making sure to keep the red dot on him, circling it so that he knew exactly where the bullet would impact him. Not a sight anyone would welcome. They took off in another direction, not going back toward the village and not heading toward the rest of our guys.

Pemberton was a few meters away from me, and since our radios weren't working, he said, "Look. There's some kind of meeting going on." He pointed over toward a dead tree where a small group of men had gathered. I watched as they turned inward and then outward toward us, pointing our way. This wasn't my call, so I got the attention of the nearest RECCE guy, Derek, a guy who had the habit of sucking in his breath loudly before saying anything.

"Let it play out. Let it play out."

I didn't respond, but I kept thinking, this is going to be really bad.

I don't know how, but Derek seemed to pick up the same vibe as me. A minute after first saying that we should let it ride, he said, "I got a bad juju about this. Let's get down. Let's really hunker down. I think an ambush is coming our way."

He was right. A few seconds later, they opened up on us from what seemed to be every direction, a 360-degree spray of AK, RPK machine gun, and pistol fire. They let loose with a few RPGs. I remembered that hole we'd seen, and so did Pemberton. We jumped up and headed toward it and Derek followed us. We managed to get into that hole. The rest of the RECCE guys, including McDonald, were pinned down around the hole. There was no way we could all fit. They'd plastered themselves as low as they could get and rounds were whizzing by our heads, so there was no way those guys could return fire. I'd gotten to the hole first, so I was at the bottom, with Pemberton and Derek both on top of me, one to my left and one to my right. They were able to lay down a few bursts of suppressive fire, but the enemy definitely had fire superiority at that moment.

I couldn't really get a fix on where the rounds were coming from. It was like we were in a blender and everything was circling around us and at some indeterminate distance. Worse, being on the bottom like that, I couldn't really see, and suddenly I felt an excruciating pain in my neck and then down toward my shoulder. At first I thought I was hit, but the pain began to dissipate and was nothing more severe than a burn. I knew then that hot brass from my guys' weapons had gotten inside my shirt.

"Let me up top! Let me up top!"

We were all in a fetal position, clustered like puppies, and were screaming at each other to see if anybody was hit.

Derek was the only guy who had somewhat active comms, but with all the chaos around us, he was having a hard time getting through. I finally managed to crawl my way to the top, and Pemberton and I were up there with Derek underneath us. I could now see, and I wished that I wasn't able to. The main unit was also coming under heavy fire. I don't know if it was ours or the Taliban's, but the sound of multiple grenades going off thumped above the main beat of our weapons. I kept thinking that we shouldn't have been doing this during the day, and I felt really bad for the second platoon guys. They were just two weeks away from being out of there and now they were caught up in this shit storm.

Even from up top I couldn't spot any targets while scanning. The stalks of native grass were being mowed down and dirt was flying all around us and that rich loamy smell of fresh earth mixed with the smell of gunpowder. About five hundred meters away, I caught some motion on top of one of the buildings. Three guys were carrying a machine gun and they were working to set it up. The firing had subsided a bit. I stuck my head up a bit higher, exposing my entire face, and a loud crack sounded. I ducked back down and Pemberton and Derek were screaming at me asking me if I was hit. I told them I was good. Another crack echoed and then the dirt right in front of Pemberton's face exploded.

"It's a sniper! It's a sniper!"

I immediately flashed back to a conversation we'd had with the marines while we were playing poker. They knew roughly where we were going and said we'd better be on our game.

"The Chechen. Watch out for that dude," one of the guys told us.

"He operates in that area. Has like three hundred kills or something."

Since I had just been Reapered and credited with that crazy number of kills, I was a little bit skeptical. The marines added that the Chechen sniper had been around since the Soviet/Afghan days.

"The dude has mad skills and a lot of kills," a marine said, setting off a round of high fives.

As I lay there in the hole with Pemberton and Derek, I remembered that line and how we'd all laughed. I wasn't laughing now. But I knew that I couldn't let that get to me.

"Pemberton, I've got three guys on top of that building setting up a machine gun nest. We've got to get some rounds on that target. I'm going after them."

"Do it. Just do it." Pemberton's voice was high-pitched and it was like you could see a cloud of adrenaline coming out of his mouth as he spoke.

We were all freaking out.

"Can you spot me?"

"I can't frickin' move. Every time I do—" He didn't have to finish the sentence. I knew that the sniper was on him.

Keeping my body pressed as tight to the ground as I could, I lifted my weapon over the edge of the hole, pushing the suppressor through the earth. With my torso pressed to the wall of the hole and my legs on its bottom, I slithered up a few inches. I was wishing I could somehow burrow underneath the ground and emerge in a new location like a worm. The next best thing was to get the barrel of my weapon up and out of the ground. I could feel it poking out. I was able to see the top of the building in the scope. I didn't have time to do any real calculations, but I guessed that they were about five hundred meters away. I squeezed off a round and it went high and right of the guy immediately behind the machine gun. I compensated for the elevation and windage and fired again. This one struck the dude right in the shoulder pocket and he went down. As soon as he did, a second Taliban fighter took up the same position, allowing me to fire again without any adjustment. He was easy, but the third guy, who had been moving forward so that he could help feed the ammo, seeing his other two guys shot dead, grabbed a few belts and took off running.

On a normal day, a guy running presented no real difficulties, but with us taking fire and everything else, all I wanted to do, if I couldn't hit him, was to get him away from that machine gun. I fired off six to eight rounds, but none of them ever struck home. Worse, as I was in that firing position, a round impacted between me and Derek. I could feel it reverberating through the ground. I rolled over toward Pemberton, and the two of us huddled together, offering whatever cover we could to each other.

"Where's he at?"

Pemberton raised his head an inch or two and another round impacted danger close. He tried another few times, but the result was the same. "Motherf---er."

The fact that the sniper was missing us made me believe that he only had a partial fix on us. He could see a hand or a foot or something, but he wasn't able to zone in on a body, otherwise one of us would have been hit.

For the first time, I was at the other end of the scope, and I didn't like it. It was driving me nuts knowing that some guy was able to fire so precisely on us. What that was doing to us mentally was pretty cruel.

I said to Derek, "We need two sets of eyes. We've got to both go up there and check for this dude's position. We both take a quick look. The machine gunners were at one o'clock. He wasn't there. Let's start there. I'll look right of that, you look left."

Our helmets were no more than three inches apart. As we both nodded that we agreed on the plan, they clanked together. I made the count. One, two, three. We raised up and took a quick look and I could feel a bullet go right between our heads. We dove back down, both of us screaming. Derek's shout was bloodcurdling and made me think he was hit. We'd made so much noise that a RECCE medic attached to us yelled in our direction, asking if we were okay. In the brief time we'd been looking for the sniper's location, I was able to see that the remaining RECCE element was lying around that field in a kind of star pattern, all of them lying with their arms and legs spread.

I looked at Derek and Pemberton and it was as if their heads had been turned inside out. It was like I could see every vein, every sinew, every tendon standing out. Their eyes were wide and their mouths hung open. Worse, I knew that what I was seeing of them was a reflection of what they were seeing in me. We were in that hole and the combined energy of our collective fear was radioactive. It was like we were in a horror movie where the nuclear fallout was peeling away our skin and revealing our insides. I tried not to think about my wife and my mom and dad, but of course, in telling myself not to think about them, I was thinking about them. I was remembering all the times since getting to Afghanistan when I thought about how cool it was that we were doing the things we had been and what it felt like when I took a guy out, and how ludicrous that all seemed to me just then. I thought of that song I'd been singing in my head—"This—sucks. This—sucks"—the cadence of it and how now it was like those words were jamming through my mind like this: "Thissucksthissucksthissucksthissucksthissucksthissucksthissucks," in one long continuous loop.

I knew that if I didn't flip that around, I was going to go nuts, and if I did, then what would that mean for the rest of the guys? I started saying to myself, "I got this." Very slowly and deliberately, and over and over so many times that I started to calm down enough to halfway believe that I was speaking the truth.

I also realized that this wasn't a situation we were going to be able to fight our way out of. Now wasn't the time to be the kid who romanticized war and thought about how cool it would be to go balls out over the top in a gung ho charge at the enemy. Now was the time for me to be the calm and calculating chess player. I had a problem to solve, a big one, and I was going to have to think things through and be a thinker and a fighter.

I accepted the fact that since I was the one who'd studied all the sniper tactics, I had to be the one to take this guy out. He was good, and what impressed me was that no one could get a fix on where he was firing from. Everything I knew about countersniping was running through my brain. This was a chess match and understanding your opponent's position, putting yourself in his shoes, was essential for success.

The army had taught us the Keep in Memory System (KIMS), and I was used to maintaining a high level of observation. I also knew that we absorbed some information subconsciously and it would come back to us if we were in a receptive state. So I was resting in that hole, closing my eyes, and alternately trying to bring back that entire scene of the village, while also thinking about where I would have chosen to position myself to do what he was attempting to do.

I recalled a building that was to the left of where the machine gunners had been. I would have chosen that. It was offset from the center of that field by about two hundred meters. Any sniper would have chosen it.

"He's in a building off to the left, Derek."

"Are you sure?"

"Hold on. Let me wait for it."

The sniper let loose with another round and I started to count. I counted to five very quickly, but the bullet landed on four. Using the snap-bang theory, I figured he was at least four hundred meters away. I took another quick look and the building I'd thought of was within that range and a window was wide open.

"That's got to be it."

The plan I worked out with Pemberton was for him to roll out of the hole and get eyes on that target—the window— and open fire with that Win Mag. Either he'd move him away from that location or maybe get lucky and get him. While he was rolling out and firing, I would also fire at that location, or in its general direction, hoping to keep him pinned down. On the count of three, we executed the move, and I started shooting. I got off three rounds and was empty. As I was reloading, I could see rounds just missing Pemberton as he did his rolls, each time the bullet striking where he'd just been.

I shook my head in admiration for the sniper. He was really good.

Pemberton hadn't been able to retrieve his weapon, but his eyesight was good enough that he reported to me that he'd seen the window and a black curtain. That had to be the location.

I tossed him his weapon, and jumped a bit when another round came danger close to me. Another impact went off near Pemberton's head. He covered his head with his arms, leaving his weapon lying nearby.

"We can't engage. We need air support."

Derek and McDonald were both feverishly working the comms to get the message out, but the second platoon was pinned down as well. They were danger close, sometimes in hand-to-hand or grenade range, depending on their location in the ravine or at the objective. They couldn't assist us.

"Are you kidding me?"

"This is bullshit."

All the guys were upset, but this was one of those situations. We could call in air support, and with a big-deal scenario like we were dealing with, we could get just about anything we needed, a B-2, an F-16 or F-15, anything at all. At least that was what I thought. One of the pilots let us know the deal.

"We cannot accept anything less than point one collateral damage. We will not be able to assist. Repeat. No assist."

The situation had gone from bad to stupid bad in that instant.

Simultaneously, the four RECCE guys with working

radios were hammering the chain of command and the pilots, cursing them out and letting them know they had no idea how bad this situation was.

"We are in the middle of an open field. Guys are about to start dying."

My radio kicked back in for a few moments, and I heard, "He's hit. He's hit. Sniper from platoon is hit."

I didn't know Walkens all that well, but anytime a guy is hit you're pissed off. Fortunately, he was struck in the foot and he was being tended to and assisted out of there. The guy was pretty salty and had been with the platoon for years; I knew that if he'd taken one, given his position, the rest of us were in deep shit.

Finally, after I jumped on comms and just pleaded our case for something, the pilots agreed to do a show of force. They were going to do a relatively low-altitude flyover and hopefully scare the crap out of those other guys with flares. I wasn't happy about that and told the team leader to just drop the bombs on us. We still had guys sprawled on the ground all around us. I could hear guys screaming, the sound of the enemy running nearby, and I knew we couldn't last much longer. I had no idea how much time had elapsed, but when I took a quick look at my watch, we'd been pinned down for nearly two hours.

I tried to skirmish my way up to Pemberton's position so that we could start to take on targets. I wasn't doing anybody any good being hunkered down in that hole. Simultaneously, our RECCE team leader rolled into the hole. I came up firing and Pemberton joined in, wearing out that building and the window we suspected the sniper fire was coming from. I told Pemberton to crank off an entire magazine, five rounds, at the window as fast as he could.

He did as I asked. While he was firing, on the fourth round, I spotted a little bit of movement in the window; the curtain the sniper used shook as the bullet passed through it. Of course, he wasn't at the window. He was somewhere back in the room firing through a small hole in the wall beneath the windowsill, doing something we called loop hold shooting. That was a tactic that had been used since the start of the war, and it was nearly impossible to counter. There was no way I could fit a round into a small space like that and hit anybody at that distance. At a hundred, two hundred, maybe three hundred meters, I had a decent chance.

Rounds kept coming in and with that sinking feeling that came with my recognition that we weren't going to be able to get him, I was just shouting blindly into my radio asking for anyone to come to our position to assist. The sniper fire had tailed off for a few minutes, and I figured he was either reloading or changing position. Didn't matter. We started to come under heavy fire again, the same 360-degree deal we'd dealt with at the start.

"Irv! Irv! I've got two guys running danger close at ten o'clock." Pemberton's voice sounded as if it was crackled with static as the sound of enemy fire snapped overhead.

"Shoot. Shoot. Shoot," was all I could manage. Then I thought I was hallucinating again. Something long and thin and black punctured the sky and came screaming overhead about five hundred feet off the ground. The shape didn't register at first, and I was thinking, UFO. It wasn't but it was close. A B-2 Stealth Bomber, with flares trailing off it, came through. It confused me, but it didn't scare me, and I knew it didn't scare our opponents. The firing never let up.

Over the comms I heard our team leader asking for bombs and the same response about point one percent collateral damage. It was starting to get comic except for the message being delivered: *We don't need a show of force. We need bombs. Guys are dying out here. Drop the bombs on us!*

I don't know what kind of damage the five hundred-pound bombs would have done to the Taliban or to us, but it didn't really matter. I wanted this thing to be over, however it ended. If nothing else, that flyover discouraged the runners, who were now veering away at six o'clock. I couldn't move at all—if I did I was sure I was going to get nailed—but Pemberton had angled his rifle toward them. The sniper was keened in on me and was using another tactic to take me on. He'd clearly figured out who I was and now I was his priority target. When you're in the situation the Chechen was in, you had a kind of checklist to go down: sniper, communications guy, medics, and so on down the line.

"One hundred meters and closing, " Pemberton said.

"How fast?"

"Jogging."

"What angle?"

"Thirty-five"

"Aim .5 mils in front of them. Hold .5 right and send it."

I heard his rifle emit its big boom.

"Missed."

"Where?"

"In front."

"Go to .2. Decrease to .2."

"Got one."

Then a moment later, Pemberton added, "I think."

"They're just standing there. Checking to see where the shot came from," McDonald added. I could see him. He'd rolled over onto his back and he was bridging his neck to look backward. "Oh, yeah, you got him."

"How can you tell?" Pemberton sounded pissed off.

"Dude's entire right side is red. That ain't normal."

We all laughed.

Pemberton fired again. "Jesus Christ on two sticks," he muttered.

"Dude," I said, "I could have hit that guy with a rock." I hoped that would ease some of the tension.

The wounded guy still hadn't gone down, and he and his buddy were walking back toward the village.

McDonald kept going with his upside-down play-by-play describing how the wounded man started staggering and his comrade took off his turban and put a tourniquet around the dude's shoulder. Pemberton and I crawled back into the hole on top of Derek. It took a few seconds for us to disentangle.

Intermittently I could still hear the transmissions indicating that we weren't going to get any assist. The team leader yelled to us and said, "I have one grenade and one smoke grenade. I can either pop smoke and we try to bound our way out or we can take this grenade and hug it."

At that moment, I think we were all feeling the same way. I could hear it in the voices of the guys over the radios and see it in the vacant looks I got from Pemberton and Derek. This was it. We were going to die. The Taliban forces were pinching in. Either we give them a fight or we hug the grenade.

Pemberton's face was inches from mine. I nodded at him, and we both smiled, wordlessly letting each other know how we felt. We bumped fists, and I felt this knot in my throat choking me.

Pemberton's expression hardened and he stared at me, as bullets smacked nearby.

"No, man. Fuck that. We're getting out of here. No way I'm facing your wife and tellin' her you died. I'm scared of her. She'd kick my ass, dude, and I can't let that happen."

I shrugged and said, "Roger that, man."

We formulated a plan. We'd use the smoke grenade as cover for us as we bounded back toward the road and a ditch that ran alongside it at our six. We'd do that in pairs.

Pemberton and I would be the last to go, so that we could continue to lay down some precision cover fire.

Just before we set the plan in motion, I did up the chinstrap of my helmet. Normally, I used to do what I called the "John Wayne" because I didn't like how the chinstrap irritated my skin. I was waiting for the countdown to when we'd pop smoke when I saw some movement over my left shoulder. I could see a small group of Rangers coming toward our position. I was able to identify one of them because of his football running style—Benjamin Kopp. He was a buddy of mine and the machine gun team leader. He was joined by a few other guys who were heavily armed with .48s and M4s. I was looking at them and had another out-of-body experience.

I watched as they came gliding in, kind of like geese in formation, and did a perfect baseball-slide landing simultaneously and took up a position. Above the sound of all the other gunfire, I could hear those machine guns pounding away. They were interlocking sectors of fire and laying waste to anything and everything in that zone, traversing those guns six inches off the ground.

I sat there listening to that sweet zinging song as the rounds passed right over our heads. I remembered as a kid we'd toss rocks at the high-tension power lines that ran through an easement in our neighborhood, and that sound like an electric guitar's D string being plucked buzzing in our bellies.

They were putting down so much gunfire, as we lay

there pressed to the earth, I felt that same vibration coming up out of the ground.

"Hell, yeah!"

"Get some!"

Derek threw the smoke grenade, but of course, the wind was against us, and it didn't do much to cover our bound back. Pemberton and I waited a bit.

"Let's do this, man."

We bumped fists and took off, running our zigzag pattern as fast as our tired legs could go. I had the sensation that I was like those kids in *E.T.* I felt like my feet weren't even touching the ground and I was rising up. Usually, with all the irrigation ditches, the rocks, and everything else, I'm pretty much a stumble-freak and fall down. Pemberton was right behind me, running half hunched over, and we slid into that ditch, me doing my best imitation of Troy Aikman sliding for a first down.

Members of the second platoon were in that ditch with us, and while I was thanking them for saving our asses, they were telling us about the grenade-tossing party they had going on.

"Dudes were picking ours up and tossing them back at us. It was nuts."

"Got to the point, we'd toss them a few feet in front of our position and hope like hell we didn't get blown up."

I could barely talk. My cheeks felt glued to my teeth and my tongue to the roof of my mouth.

I barely managed to squeak a request for water. I drank half the bottle and tossed the rest to Pemberton. After that, I told the guys that we needed to pick it up and get to a safe house. We formed up with Pemberton and me at the rear. Suddenly it went all quiet.

As the movement began, I saw out of my peripheral vision a man in white clothing peeking from behind a corner of a nearby hut. I called Pemberton over to me and laid my rifle on his shoulder. I told him to inhale and then exhale, timing my breaths with his, making sure that I could compensate for the rising and falling of the gun's barrel. As soon as my eye focused on the scope reticule, the man popped out pointing an AK-47 barrel in our direction. I squeezed the trigger immediately as the center of my crosshairs landed on his chest. His body crumpled under his dead weight, partially exposing his head from the corner of the building, with the AK-47 lying underneath him. Pemberton jumped when I fired, and who could blame him with my weapon being so close to his ear.

"Got him, dude. Let's go."

We made our way to the front by doing something stupid. We took a route right up against the tree line. All it did was silhouette us against that backdrop. I didn't know what the Chechen was up to, but I'd given him a huge opportunity. I guess we were more interested in speed than safety at that point, so I relied on the old geometry lesson about the shortest distance between two points. I wanted to get over to help the guys in second platoon since they'd bailed us out. Gunfire, from maybe fifty meters away, was coming in on us. Another ambush. We made a left turn and I could see, all along my left side, heads popping out of the ground. Vietnam. These guys had freakin' fighting tunnels.

To our right was a ditch, and I cartwheeled headfirst into the muddy water. I came up spluttering in the chest-deep water, while all around me guys were returning fire helter-skelter in the direction we thought the shots had come in from. I put my rifle up on the embankment and looked through the scope. It was coated with mud, I was dripping wet, and now, my intermittent radio was completely dead due to drowning. I cleaned the sight as best I could and began scanning.

I heard the report of a rifle and a snapping sound right next to me. I thought whoever was next to me was way too close, but I looked over, no one was there. The sounds coming from my left were the supersonic snaps passing close to my ear and impacting the mud wall behind me. I now knew for sure the Chechen was still out there, and as I moved to my right, each of his shots grew closer and closer to hitting me.

Firing off another shot and hitting an enemy Taliban in the face, I looked back to my left and prepared to move away from my targeted location. I saw Kopp, half in and half out of the ditch, his right foot up on the embankment, and he was firing away. I heard another strange sound, but not the sound of a bullet snapping overhead; this was a different sound, like someone slapping a ruler against a pillow. That was followed by a loud scream. Kopp, one of the men who came in to save us just a few minutes ago, had been struck in the thigh. A stream of blood sprayed out from his leg and into the water. He was screaming that he was hit and cursing. A couple of guys dove on top of him and then began applying pressure on his wound. Blood quickly filled the stagnant water that we were in, turning the water a dark, reddish brown. Pemberton and I and a few M4 and machine gunners raised ourselves out of the water and emptied our magazines on the partially obscured enemy.

While we were engaging, one of our medics, Melvin, a big black guy, ran under heavy incoming fire and through waist-deep water to reach Kopp. Upon reaching him, Melvin tossed his medical bag into the water, opened it and proceeded to provide care. I was in complete awe watching the medic go to work with his medical bag floating in the ravine and bullets impacting all around him.

We had to get the hell out of there. I turned around and the platoon leader (PL) was behind me. I shouted, "Do you want us to move up and secure your entry to the Alamo?" I was referring to the name of the safe house. He couldn't hear me, so I pulled him close. Then, I felt what seemed to be water smack the side of my face.

It wasn't water; it was blood.

The PL sank from my grasp and into the water, screaming, "I'm hit, I'm hit!" A single round had struck the PL in the upper chest, just above his body armor. I was so stunned by the fact that a bullet had just missed me and struck the PL that I could barely move. Pemberton immediately fell on the PL and placed his finger in the bullet hole while I turned back to my rear and emptied half a magazine toward the enemy. A medic from my recon team ran over to assist the PL. The damned sniper had strategically taken out key members of our team and was still focusing in on Pemberton and me.

Something clicked in me, and I got up onto level ground and just started firing every time I saw a head come up. I saw one split in two. I was doing nothing but engaging and engaging until I had to reload. I sank back down and the medic had a compress on the PL's wound and an IV stuck in his arm.

"Get that son of a bitch. Get that son of a bitch," the PL kept saying to me, looking glassy-eyed but determined.

"I'm trying. I'm trying." More rounds seemed targeted at me and were smacking into the back of the embankment.

"Everybody else okay? You got to get out of here."

I saw Derek and he lifted his chin, signaling me to come closer to him. I low-crawled toward him and he said, "I'm not taking any fire at all."

As soon as I raised myself up a bit, a bullet flew between us.

Derek's eyes grew wide. "He's locked in on you. Get down. Get down."

I worked back to my previous spot while Derek fired.

We all knew we had to get out of there.

Another of the team leaders asked Melvin how much more time he needed to stabilize Kopp.

Melvin didn't turn toward us for a full five to ten seconds. When he did, he didn't need to say a word. We all knew that his expression was telling us that it wasn't going to matter how much time he spent. Things weren't looking too good for Kopp.

By that time, Kopp had stopped his screaming and was lying there shaking his head slowly from side to side. Guys were telling him, "Hey dude, you're doing okay. You're doing okay."

I looked down and I could see two blood-soaked gauze pads floating in the water like little square life rafts. Melvin had already applied two tourniquets and was pressing a third gauze pad to the wound. It was like watching a paper towel soaking up a red spill.

Guys came up with a makeshift litter and placed Kopp in it. He was likely bleeding out, but we had to get him to a field hospital somehow and hope for the best.

The team leader shook his head.

"Let's go. Screw it. Right now."

The PL no longer had his shirt on and had his body armor draped over him like a cape. He was holding the gauze to Kopp's chest. And he started slogging through the water with the rest of us. Pemberton and I volunteered to grab Kopp's gear to make carrying him easier. Pemberton stuck with me, and we leaned back as Kopp was carried past us. The water varied in depth quite a bit, and just as he got even with us, Kopp's face disappeared under the water for a moment and then rose again. He'd gone bone-white pale and his face was now slack, but I could see his chest rising and falling in small spasms of breath. We were still taking fire, and the guys carrying him had to keep low.

Finally, Pemberton and I started half swimming, half low-crawling out of that ditch. I could barely move. I kept waiting for some Taliban guy to jump into the ditch and strafe us all. I was kind of wishing that would happen. My legs and arms were cramping so bad, I just wanted to lie down in that water or have someone shoot me. I kept thinking of Kopp being dunked like that and the calm expression on his face.

Pemberton sensed that something had changed in me. I felt as if the mud that was sucking my boots and caking on my skin was stealing the life out of me. I knew that Kopp's chances weren't good, and we'd been close. None of this seemed worth it. Pemberton was a few meters ahead of me, and he turned and said, "Suck it up. You're a Ranger. Let's finish this thing."

No sooner had we gotten near the safe house than we were instructed to move to the front of the line. We needed to lay down suppressive fire while the wounded were placed inside. My clothes were now so heavy and stiff all I could do was a Frankenstein shuffle into position. My rifle looked like it had been dipped in chocolate and left to harden. I searched my pockets and found a kaffiyeh, a scarf that I'd picked up in Iraq, and used it to clean my optics as best I could. I also realized that I was down to my last two mags of ammo, and one of them was caked in mud.

"Here we go," I said to Pemberton. "This is going to suck."

We had about fifty meters of open ground to cover before we could reach the building. We climbed up onto the top of the embankment and sat there for a second taking a tactical pause. I figured the sniper was nearby and this was going to be another chance to get shot at.

I set out at a sprint, and about halfway home an outrageous burst of gunfire started going off. I dropped down to the ground, and a second later, Pemberton had grabbed me by the shoulders while kneeling beside me. Once he was sure I wasn't hit, he finally responded to what I'd been saying, to get down, we were taking fire.

"No. No. We're not. Those are our guys."

I laughed a bit and we got up and started running. There were six Rangers from the assault force on a rooftop firing every gun they had in their arsenal. The sounds of 7.62 and 5.56 machine guns unleashing all at once no more than eight feet over our heads caused the ground to shake. I thought we had been ambushed by an army of Taliban.

Once inside the safe house, we came up to two fifteen-foot-tall French doors, blue with a white cow painted on them. The cow had a lei around its neck. I shouldered past the cow and there inside was the main element we'd started out with who knew how many hours before.

We finally got some good news. They'd taken out the target we were initially after, a few other guys besides, and there in the middle of floor, flex-cuffed together, was a group of Taliban fighters and leaders. They looked up at me; I looked at them, and then I turned to the first sergeant.

"Get high up. We need the snipers to pick these guys off!" he instructed us.

These were the words I had been waiting to hear all day.

Pemberton and I ran over to the nearby mud house and climbed a ladder on the rear side that one of the locals had left behind. The men who had lain down covering fire met us with smiling faces and a large pile of smoking-hot brass around them.

"Dudes. That was unreal."

They all smiled and one said, "I've never fired that many rounds on target. It was awesome."

The sun had now reached its highest point and the temperature was above 120 degrees. The bottom of my combat boots started to torch my feet as I lay down behind my rifle, observing targets in the distance. As much as it burned, the overwhelming number of targets I was now able to see through my 10 power scope shut out all other feeling.

I wasn't sure what would happen if I shot my rifle after it had been submerged. *Screw it,* I thought. The first bullet I let out reminded me of firing a Super Soaker squirt gun. It didn't leave a vapor trail so much as it let out a trail of water. The bullet hit a wall, nowhere near where I was aiming. Pemberton was sitting on the ground spitting on bullets and wiping them off on his shirt.

I focused in on a target almost half a mile from our position, carrying an AK-47, with ammo draped over his shoulder. I wasn't sure how much I had to lead him with my scope because I wasn't sure how fast he was running. Pemberton was busy working on a target with his .300 Win Mag and I didn't want to bother him.

I figured I would lead my target by 3.5 mils to start off with, and watch the impact of the bullet as it hit the ground, which would allow me to make a correction. I reached up and dialed 23 minutes of angle on the elevation of the scope. With each click I made on the scope, the target began to slow down. As his pace came to a halt, a slight grin grew on my face. "I got you now," I thought out loud. Slowly pulling the trigger back as the center of my reticule lay on the center of his chest, I noticed the heat mirage pick up at a steep angle. Before the shot broke, I adjusted for the wind indicated by the mirage.

As the shot broke, I saw the tail end of the vapor trail from the bullet fly downrange and sink into the target's upper chest cavity. The bullet hit him with such force it caused his man dress to fly open, exposing the bullet wound. The impact looked like an eighteen-wheeler truck going a hundred miles an hour had hit him. His rifle flew from his hands as he fell backward into the powdery dirt.

As fast as he hit the dirt, two of his friends came in to retrieve his body and drag it off behind a small mud hut. I didn't engage the men. Instead I shifted my scope to the left, focusing at a long road. I could see groups of men exiting a white vehicle, all carrying AK-47s. The distance was too far for me to engage them so I shouted over to Pemberton, "Hey, hit the guys in the white car!"

I knew that the shot would be a tough one. It was over a kilometer, but I figured the sound of a .300, 190 grain bullet snapping in their direction would keep them out of the fight.

"Medevac is in route!" someone shouted to us. The army's best helicopter pilots were coming in to extract the wounded. My team on the roof continued to engage the enemy to the best of our abilities for hours, at most utilizing suppressive fire. We had to keep focus on the amount of ammo we had with each shot we put downrange. It got to the point where I asked one of the machine gunners to take off a strip of ten rounds from his belt of ammo hanging from his MK-48. The rounds were becoming scarce, and a whole new fear set in.

I wanted to see the guys before they were medevaced out of there. Wilkins, a sniper team leader from 2nd platoon, was up against a wall with his wounded leg out in front of him. The PL was getting treatment, and I saw the stretcher that Kopp had been carried in on. He wasn't in it, but I could see that it was soaked with blood. I stood there staring at that, and one of the guys nodded toward a back room. I didn't want to go back there. I'd seen how Kopp had looked and I preferred carrying that image with me to what I might see. I took a few sips of water, and headed back out onto the roof of the far building.

Over the tops of the trees in the distance, I could see the medevac hauling in. As the helicopter approached, we shifted fire to avoid sending a stray round in their direction. Even under the AK-47 fire, the helicopter landed in between our position and the enemy, absorbing any potential incoming rounds as a few men carried and assisted the three wounded rangers. As quickly as they came in, they were off, flying them to the nearest hospital. As for us, the fight continued.

"ALLAHU AKBAR!"

I quickly looked over my shoulder behind me and over the tall wall that surrounded the house. There were four men that had managed to get within a few feet from the outside of the wall. They were so close that I could see the features on their faces and the dirt smudged under their eyes. I got the attention of the guys on the roof and signaled to them that we would take them out all at once before they were able to gain entry. "I got the guy in the checkered shirt!" I yelled to my guys. They all quickly replied back to me, identifying which target they had.

"I got left."

"I got right."

"I got center."

"Three, two, one . . ." With one loud *BOOM,* the targets crumbled and fell to the ground as they were all engaged. I remember the target being so close in my scope that I could see the detail in one of his buttons on his shirt as I squeezed the trigger.

"Immediate extract needed! Immediate extract needed our location!" came over the net, calling to a Marine FOB nearby.

"Negative. You guys have to come to us. We cannot go into that area with anything less than a brigade. We will position near your location south. Over," the marines responded.

"Let's get ready to move out, boys!"

I was in disbelief. We had been in the area with a small team of Rangers in a firefight from hell, surrounded, and at some points almost overrun. At times we were forty strong and at other times only six strong. Now they couldn't come in there with less than a brigade?

The plan for our extraction was as simple as it could get. We had to run to the marines in Humvees waiting for us on a nearby hill overlooking our location almost a mile away! I remember thinking to myself in a sarcastic tone, *I swear I've seen this before . . . oh, yeah,* Black Hawk Down."

As my team climbed down from the rooftop and gathered with the remaining Rangers on the ground, Pemberton and I checked our magazines to see how much ammo we had left. We were both down to our last mag. Pemberton had around twelve rounds left while I was down to my last ten out of the two hundred-plus rounds we each started off with. All I could imagine was running through the enemy, engaging them in hand-to-hand combat, stabbing them with the large six-inch Buck knife I carried on my hip.

"Irv, can you put your snipers in front and behind our formation?" the commander asked.

"Roger."

Being the sniper squad/team leader, I wanted to take the front and have Pemberton pick up the six. I have to admit, I was a little nervous about what might lie in the open terrain leading to the marines. The pucker factor was maxed out.

The large blue doors opened and I started to run. My body was drained not only from the five-day operation but also the now half-day-long firefight we were in. Every time my boot hit the soft dirt, I would look at a different sector, observing where any potential enemy could be. With the sound of the bullets snapping overhead, my pace picked up. The vomit rising in my throat from overexertion was suppressed by the sight of the awaiting Humvees.

"Get in, get in, get in!" we shouted, arriving at the vehicles. The expressions the marines had on their faces were almost indescribable. It seemed as if they thought we were crazy for going into the area.

With the captured targets in hand, we packed ourselves in the Humvees like sardines. An entire Ranger assault force and recon/sniper team was stuffed in four Humvees already packed with marines. I had managed to cram myself under the feet of the marine .50 cal gunner with my head resting on my spotter's knee and my body folding on Nate, another sniper. The pain I felt from being crushed didn't bother me, I was just happy we were getting out.

But, man, I wanted a cigarette so bad. I bummed one from the .50 cal gunner. Once I got down to the filter, I tried to flick the butt out of the hatch. I immediately regretted that decision when I felt the skin of my neck starting to sizzle. Nate started slapping me, trying to put that butt out. Then he doused me with his water bottle.

All I could do was laugh.

"Some day, huh?" my personal fireman said.

Before I could answer, I heard enemy rounds pinging off the Humvee.

"It ain't over yet," I said, thinking that now I was going to have to bum some ammo off these guys.

7. A Whole 'Nother Danger

As painful as it had been to be crammed into that Humvee, I was grateful that we were no longer being shot at. I'd been under fire before, but our firefights seldom lasted very long and we so frequently outgunned our opponents that the action was over in a matter of minutes. July 10, 2009, was by far the longest day of my life and the longest firefight I'd ever been involved in. I didn't want to ever come close to breaking that record.

When we rejoined our platoon, we took our captives and separated them from one another. After a very short debrief, I was assigned to oversee one of the prisoners. Our emotions were still running high as the rest of the guys talked about what had just happened. It was like we had to keep telling ourselves the stories over and over again to make sense of what had taken place. One of the craziest things that I saw, and what really shocked me, was that everybody on the operation had multiple bullet holes through their clothing. Our body armor had done its thing and we didn't even feel the impacts. Maybe that had to do with adrenaline pumping as well. Things got so intense during the fighting that our combat cameraman even picked up a weapon, something, as a general rule, they don't do. Even though I hadn't really slept more than a few minutes, maybe an hour or so total, over the course of those ninety-six or so hours, I was still too jazzed to sleep.

Finally, though, when we were waiting for transport via Chinooks, I drifted off. Just as soon as I nodded off, though, I heard a loud crack go past my ear. I immediately jumped up, put on my rucksack and stood there looking around, surveying the scene. All I saw was the rest of the guys just sitting there as calm as could be. In my head, bullets were still flying; in reality they weren't.

Our team of six was going to fly back separately. Second platoon was going to return to FOB Bastion. We'd formed a bond with all those guys, but now they were leaving, and in a short time they were going back home. We shook hands and congratulated each other, but you could tell that reality was starting to set in and to set in hard. Kopp was seriously wounded. Several guys were wounded. For a while, none of us wanted to be alone with our thoughts, but now, as the Chinook that was to take us back to our compound was landing, it was like the truth was setting in.

On the flight back, I thought of Kopp, hoped that somehow he was going to be okay. I also thought of another guy we all knew back in sniper section. Santiago was a little

Hispanic guy who we all really liked. He was only five foot four or five inches tall, but he was the dad of the entire sniper section. He was older than all of us, had done his time in the navy and then as a Chicago policeman. In his thirties, he was the lowest-ranked guy, but you would have never known that considering how much we all looked up to him. He was a sniper/spotter, but he didn't have the same kind of training background as most of the guys. One of the snipers, Harris, met Santiago, liked him, knew that he was a squared-away guy and chose him to be a sniper.

Santiago worked his butt off. I thought that getting to work every morning between five-thirty and six was a killer, but Santiago would show up at three or four. He'd come in before anyone else got there and take care of almost all of our administrative work. None of us wanted to deal with paperwork, and Santiago knew that, so he took it on for the rest of us. He'd also stay late, and we'd tell him to get out of there too, but he'd stay and do even more tasks for us, like checking and lubing the ladders and helping maintain a lot of the other gear.

I can't say that we took advantage of him though. He was trying to catch up on some training, so he'd ask us for help. Once, after everybody else was gone, he walked outside with me and asked me to help him scale a building. This was free-climbing. I don't really know why, maybe because I had to do so much work at heights, but my fear of them was mostly gone. I loved free-climbing. To me, it was like a chess match, figuring out the best foot- and hand-holds.

We were all pretty tight in the unit and we'd established an informal chain of command in case one of us got killed or seriously wounded. We called it our secret red alert. We'd be as factual as possible and tell all the wives what had gone down. That way, they could be there for the other women who were hurting. We knew that we could rely on each other, and so could they. When any of the guys in the platoon got hurt, we'd all get together. Sometimes we'd all just sit and watch the video footage. Somehow seeing how it happened made us feel better. That was because what we saw was real and not some image that we had mixed up in our minds.

For me, watching the live video feeds served another purpose. Pemberton and I always wanted to be out there helping when we saw our guys in any kind of trouble. We'd get flown in and try to take care of business as best we could. When you're in battalion for a long time, those bonds are strong. A lot of us came into battalion at the same time, so we grew up together. A lot of the guys who'd seen early deployments to Iraq and Afghanistan had decided they'd had enough and retired. Some of the Rangers opted out by going on to Green Beret or Delta Force as well. The turn-over was pretty significant so even though I was fairly young in terms of age, I was fairly senior in terms of years.

I didn't become a sniper team leader right away. I'd failed my first exam and I needed to pass in order to become an E5—to be honest I just didn't put in the study time needed. I was going through four different sniper schools and that ate up most of my study time. The guys at the board must have seen that, and they allowed me to take the test again. Right before my deployment in 2009, I was named team leader.

I didn't ever really think too much about whether or not I deserved it. I felt like I had the experience in the field but I know that I didn't know a whole lot about leadership. That's the thing though. When you know you don't know something, and you don't act like you know it, people respect you. In some ways it was like being a coach for a professional team. If you've played the game at the pro level, the guys on the team automatically give you a pass—at least for a little while. After all, you'd become a Ranger and that was worth some respect up front. It was weird for me being only twenty-two and having to lead guys who were older than me. Maybe that's why I wasn't so strict about using rank and all that.

When the six of us who'd gone out on that original recon mission returned, we came home to something I didn't expect. Everybody was out near our briefing room, fully kitted out ready to go out on an operation. Frick, one of the machine gunners and a guy who looked like he'd taken a leave of absence from his NFL team where he was a star linebacker, was the first guy to walk up to us.

We bumped fists and I asked him, "What's going on? You got a mission?"

"Did have, but you guys made it back."

"What do you mean?"

"Irv, we were coming out to get you guys. All the shit you were in, we couldn't just sit here watching it go down."

It seemed like at that point nearly everybody in the platoon came up and said something, patted us on the shoulder, or did something to acknowledge what we'd been through. To a man they talked about how watching the drone imagery was one of the coolest things they'd seen.

Benson, a college guy who'd walked away from a Wall Street job, put it best. "All those images needed was a soundtrack and I was back in the multiplex. I was willing to order popcorn for the whole platoon. That was insane. Seeing you guys come out of those blue doors and run through all that gunfire, that was unbelievable, Francis Ford Coppola shit."

Everybody was happy we'd made it out and, as had happened before, some of the guys expressed their jealousy. As bad as things were, as dangerous as it had all been, they wanted to be in on it. That's part of the mentality, wanting to prove yourself under fire. You spent all those hours undergoing exhausting training, and when you don't get to see how you'd perform under the pressure of the real thing, jealousy is a genuine and understandable response. Having gone through that longest day, I wouldn't have wished that experience on my own worst enemy. I tried to tell a few guys that, but I don't think they really got it. Maybe they thought I was trying to build it up into something even more horrible than it was, but there were multiple times when I was scared out of my mind. I couldn't really tell them that, or tell them about the feelings of just wanting it all to be over, but those moments were real.

I tried not to think too much about the Chechen, but in the days that followed I was still haunted by him. It's one thing to come under fire. That's a random act of violence and is what most of war is about. It's just some guy on their side firing at you because your guys are firing at him. What I experienced was personal. Seeing sniper action from the other side made me realize how calculating the act was. Though neither of us had gone out there that day knowing that we'd be targets ourselves, that was how it had played out—for me especially. Lots of people think of war as being between armies and governments or between this platoon and that unit, but it really does sometimes come down to one guy with a gun and another guy with a gun.

Shredding a location with a machine gun is one thing. Firing artillery rounds or dropping bombs on a position is another. I'd been a deliverer of death: the Reaper who came and collected lives. Being the target of someone else's reaping wasn't something I'd ever even considered before that day. We'd trained to respond to sniper attacks, but that always felt like a remote, beyond-worst-case-scenario contingency, something like quadratic equations you'd learn in school, something with no application in your real life.

We all, I think, tried to make death an abstract reality. That's a contradiction, but we knew it was out there, kind of like a tornado or some other freakish part of nature that was no use spending too much time thinking about. Living in Maryland, we didn't even do tornado drills as school kids, the chances of one churning up were that remote. So what I guess I was left with was thunderstorms and the possibility of being struck by lightning, and how rare was that? Even though I was in the stormiest place in the war, I still felt like death was random. Now I started wondering if maybe I was on the enemy's radar, a recognizable threat that needed to be taken out.

I had another more immediate concern. I smelled like death, that ammonia smell that comes from not having showered for a week. The rest of the guys were preparing to stand down for the night, and Pemberton and I were standing there like a couple of zombies. Our platoon sergeant, Casey, came up to us and he put his hands on us.

"I don't want to get too close and catch whatever funk it is you got."

We all laughed.

"We were worried about you guys. Helluva day out there. You guys showed some balls though. Proud of you. Ranger proud."

Pemberton and I mumbled our thanks.

"But seriously, man, you guys smell like Mrs. Satan's vagina. Get a shower."

"Roger that."

Pemberton and I shuffled off to our rooms. We shrugged off our packs and left our weapons in a storage room. We stripped in the hallway, not wanting to bring our clothes and our smell into our rooms. The fluorescent lights in the hallway always messed with my vision, but in my sleep-deprived state, everything seemed liquid and wavering as I made my way to the shower room. I can't express what that shower felt like. Pemberton and I didn't talk at all. I know we found comfort in being together, and having gone through that experience together applied more cement to our bond. At one point, standing with my head down and the water beating down on my neck and shoulders, I was shaking uncontrollably. At first I thought maybe the hot water had run out, but then I realized it was my body shutting down or signaling me in some way that it had had enough.

I racked out for eighteen hours, interrupted only by a couple of guys knocking on the door to deliver some chow. I was so tired an empty Gatorade bottle became my urinal. I was hurting down to my bones, and the last time I'd felt that kind of muscle and mental fatigue was in Ranger school. Pemberton and I were stood down for three days to allow us to recuperate. Somewhere somebody had secured two lawn chairs and they donated them to our cause. We

sat up there on our balcony cleaning all our gear and prepping for our next operation.

Fortunately for us, there was a bit of a lull. That serious
engagement had taken place on July 10 of 2009. I was so
out of it at the time, you could have told me that it had
taken place on Thanksgiving Day. I remember the next
important date very well, and I wish I didn't.

Pemberton and I were baking on the balcony, getting
a little bit of fresh air after too many hours in the air-
conditioning. Platoon Sergeant Casey walked up. I didn't
know Casey all that well, except that this was going to be
his last deployment. He was a good guy, not too gung ho
or by the book and not so fast and loose that you didn't really
respect him. Like me, he was from a military family, from
somewhere out west. He had the habit, like a gunslinger
out of the old west, of squinting whenever he spoke, even
indoors. This time, I noticed no sign of his trademark expression.

The skin of his face hung slack. "I thought you guys
would want to know. Kopp. He didn't make it."

Kopp had been airlifted out of Afghanistan and on to
Germany and then home to the U.S. It had been eight
days, and though it wasn't completely a case of out of sight
out of mind, with each day that passed without any news of
him, we assumed that he was recovering. For a few moments, I had that same feeling I'd had while being pinned

down in that ditch by the Chechen. I tried to shift mental and emotional positions, but always came up hurting.

"Goddamn," Pemberton said. He rested his chin in his hands and I watched as he worked his jaw side to side.

"I'm sorry, Sergeant," I said. I knew that he was taking the loss hard. As a platoon sergeant, he felt responsible for all his guys, and being so close to the end of his series of deployments, losing somebody was especially tough.

"Bronze Star. Purple Heart. Meritorious Service Medal. All of them." Casey listed those awards as if he was talking about a prison sentence. I knew what he was feeling. Kopp deserved them all, but we wished that he had been able to earn them some other way.

I wouldn't learn this until after I got back, but Kopp committed another act of sacrifice and heroism. He was an organ donor and his heart went to a woman in Chicago, a fifty-seven-year-old woman who's going to be able to live out her days peaceably and productively thanks to Benjamin Kopp. He put his life on the line, as did all of the guys from Company C and Third Battalion. I knew that he was a single guy, and I wondered how his mom and dad were handling the bad news. I wanted to give Jessica a call and maybe have her contact my mom and dad to see if they could let his mom and dad know that there were a bunch of guys who owed their son and them an enormous debt.

While Pemberton and I sat there quietly shaking our

heads, Sergeant Casey walked off, his head down, the weight of Kopp's death clearly on him. He stopped and said, over his shoulder, "If you guys need anything, let me know."

We spent the next hour or so sitting in silence, thinking. None of the other guys came up to us, giving us space to grieve. We went to chow and ate mechanically because that's what bodies do, mostly; they keep going on.

Not that Sergeant Casey could have ordered this up for us, but we got exactly what we needed to get our minds off Kopp. A few hours later, our pagers went off and we were in the briefing room. This appeared to be a basic operation, a capture or kill of a Taliban leader, a local who'd been providing intel. The only wrinkle was that our insertion point was going to be in the middle of a very large irrigation field. As a result of all the ditches, the pilots wouldn't be able to land. When I heard that, I started to grin. That meant one thing: fast roping. I had only done it once since training—in combat in Iraq.

For a guy who had a fear of heights, you'd think fast roping out of a helicopter hovering forty or so feet above the ground would be terrifying. For some reason, I thought that fast roping was going be a piece of cake in comparison to what we'd been through. We'd spent so much time in irrigation fields since we'd arrived that it felt completely natural to be in one. Fast-rope descents are a classic case of in control verging on being out of control. Fractured or sprained limbs were a possibility, but I loved the feeling of being on that edge as I descended. At least that was what I tried to tell myself.

At the briefing, I laid out Pemberton's and my positioning plan. There weren't any buildings nearby where a high angle would be advantageous, so we decided that we were to sit off to one side of the target's residence. From there we'd have a good view through a large gate. We'd have easy access to the structure's main door and its windows. We should be able to have eyes on the target as well as our guys as they made their way into the small compound.

As we packed up, we broke out for the first time our pairs of heavy leather gloves. They were useless for anything but fast roping as far as I was concerned, but invaluable in helping you to hang on and to halt your ascent. With all my gear on, I weighed pretty close to two hundred pounds or more. I was used to carrying that much weight when on two feet, but you start moving somewhere around the $10.2 \, \text{m/s}^2$ that our friend, and sometime enemy, Mr. Gravity pulled us down at, and that extra weight really mattered. We would exit out of the back of the Chinook, not first but near the beginning of the group, and I wanted to make sure that Pemberton and I would be next to each other, leaving at the same time on one of the two ropes.

After the crew chiefs made sure the ropes were secure, we were in the air. Forty or so minutes later we got the one-minute signal. The entire ride in, my bravado regarding fast roping was being ripped to shreds by the wind passing by the Chinook. All that was left of my optimistic kite was a couple of very fragile sticks of balsa wood. All kinds of negative thoughts started running through my mind. I was sure I was going to biff it on the landing and get hurt. I had that bladder-buzzing, gut-knotted sensation that was once reserved for doing oral reports in school.

When the Chinook decelerates, it feels like the engines are going to shake the bird apart. We stood up and I don't know if my body's shaking and its harmonics matched the Chinook's, but I walked pretty steadily forward. Pemberton was alongside me as the first few guys stepped out. We fist-pounded and the next thing I knew I was off the ramp. It was nighttime, of course, but through the darkness I could see that this was no ordinary irrigation field. Those little ditches, the ones where I'd pressed my body down into the earth for fear that parts of me would be exposed, had been replaced by little canyons with dirt mounded up alongside them. It was like I was at the pyramids or something, wondering who the hell did this and how the hell these things got built. Another question came crashing in; what were these things for?

All that wondering had taken my mind off the job at hand—getting down that rope. I was so uncertain of what kind of surface we were landing on that I was holding on too tight and not maintaining my space discipline. I knew the guy above could come crashing down on top of me if I didn't pick it up and soon. There was no way to be heard above the hurricane roar of wind the Chinook produced. I kept looking down at these deep trenches and the piles beside them, knowing that the rope only went down so far, and most likely not to the very bottom of those holes. I didn't want to have to jump into one of them. I could see a couple of guys below, looking very antlike on those hills and holes.

Finally, I touched solid earth, or more or less solid ground. The clumps and loose earth gave way beneath my feet. Fortunately, Pemberton was right nearby. We each prepped our weapons and started to maneuver our way up to the top of one of the ditches. Thankfully, there was what seemed to be a continuous ridge we could walk on. Going up and down and up and down and in and out of those ditches would have exhausted us and consumed every second before daylight.

This was bizarre and I felt like we'd been dropped onto the surface of a different planet. I tried to remember the maps and whether the topographical details we'd looked at matched up to what we were now facing. Was I too preoccupied by the prospect of fast roping that I hadn't paid close enough attention? Was Kopp's death weighing too heavily on my mind?

Something told me I better check myself and not let my thoughts wander too much. We all made it through that first section. I kept my eyes on different features of the terrain, thinking that some of them would have been good hides for a sniper. With everyone safely down, the Chinook departed, and we had to cover four to five hundred meters to get to the objective within a tiny village. I realized that we were walking on a kind of ledge. To our right were some deep ditches, not at all like the shallow ones we'd normally encountered. They weren't so deep that you'd kill yourself if you fell or get seriously hurt, but it would be a huge pain in the ass to have to climb back out of them. To our left was blackness, a kind of shadow that seemed to encompass an enormous area. It reminded me of an open doorway to a darkened room or the entrance to a cave.

The plan called for us to make our way to the low wall that surrounded the village and stack up against it. From there, we'd break off and do our thing. Two other snipers, Perkins and Jillian, had asked to join us, and they'd gotten the okay. They had been dropped off by another Chinook and taken up their position on the opposite side of the compound and across from the house our target was in. I had only walked maybe sixty or so meters of that ledge when something told me to take out my ear protection. I'd been fighting a battle with those little pieces of foam my entire career, but after that most recent engagement, we'd called a mutual cease-fire. I'd been able to get through that horrible day with them in, and with us firing so many rounds in such close quarters, I knew that my eardrums would have been a casualty for sure if it weren't for their intervention. I pulled them out and stowed them in my pocket.

Because of the position we were going to take, Pemberton and I were at the back of the formation. I could hear the guys' footsteps scraping and crackling on the loose gravel, but once I'd stopped walking, those sounds receded. Pemberton was pulling up the rear. I'd done a head count with him a couple of times before I'd stopped and he was there each time.

I'd just passed the boundary of that enormous shadow, and as I was standing there, I heard, very faint but very distinctly, the hard consonant sounds of my first name: *ck—ck*.

I wondered what the hell that could be. It was clearly a human-made sound. I looked back over my shoulder to ask Pemberton if he heard it and my heart dropped. Pemberton wasn't there.

I had to walk myself through the situation. I was in front of Pemberton. Pemberton was behind me. It would have been impossible for him to pass me without me seeing him. I moved forward and tapped the shoulder of the guy in front of me, Atkins, the platoon sergeant.

"Stay here for a minute."

"What's up?"

"I'm going back a ways. I heard something. Pemberton's not behind me."

I walked back along that edge, fighting a rising panic. I

went maybe thirty meters or so, in the middle of that black shadow that was now to my right. The ledge was maybe four feet wide, but for some reason, I stepped slightly into the shadow. The shadow wasn't a shadow at all, but an enormous hole, approximately forty feet in diameter. I looked down and my heart dropped into that blackness. It wasn't just my fear of heights but the certainty that Pemberton was down there. Who knew how far down, but he wasn't visible. It was so dark in there, seemingly like what I'd read and seen about black holes in outer space. To put it mildly, I was freaked out. It really was like the earth had swallowed up Pemberton and now it was sitting there with its mouth wide open mocking me, saying, "Look. I don't have him."

"Mike," I whispered hoarsely. It was as if the hole chewed up those vibrations. It was a weird sensation to realize my voice was not carrying very far at all. I seldom used Pemberton's first name, and it registered with me that I had.

I tried his comms, but got no response.

I couldn't contain myself anymore, and, breaking every bit of mission protocol, I shouted at the top of my lungs, "M-i-i-i-i-k-k-e!"

I was so freaked out I would have laughed when I heard his voice rising up out of that pit of blackness, coming to me as calm as could be, "Hey, what's up, man. Yeah, I'm down here. I need you to come get me."

I could feel relief washing over me, cooling my armpits. I

had no idea what could have happened to him, but knowing that he could talk to me made me feel so much better.

"Okay. I'm going to dekit and take my body armor off. I'll be lightweight and I'm going to jump down there and get you out. You still got your ladder?"

"Yeah, man. I still got it. It's on my back."

"I'll get down there and I'll help you set up the ladder and we'll climb out. How far down are you?"

"Ten feet. Maybe fifteen. It's hard to tell."

Only now, as I recount this exchange, do I realize how I was assuming that because he could talk to me that he was fine. He didn't sound like he was in pain, he didn't say anything about whether he was hurting at all. I had one thought in my mind—get him out of there and continue on our way to the objective.

With our capture-or-kill mission in mind, I got in contact with Sergeant Casey, and again, I should have thought more before speaking.

"We've got a man down."

"Say again!"

"We've got a man down."

"I didn't hear any weapons fire."

"No. No. Negative. We have a man down in a hole."

"Roger that. Get him out."

I turned to another team member Trambley and said, "Just to be safe, let's get that fast rope we came in on. We can drop it down there in case the ladder won't reach."

Thinking quickly, Trambley looked at me and said, "Wait a second." He took out a chemical light, cracked it, and dropped it down the hole. We stood there watching as that little glow dropped and then disappeared completely.

"Oh my God," I said.

"Holy shit." Trambley's eyes were wide and his mouth hung open.

My heart was outracing my thoughts. I knew I needed to remain calm, but my buddy was down there somewhere, who knew how far, and I had no idea how we were going to get him back up here.

To confirm what I'd just witnessed, I picked up a small pebble and dropped it down, hoping that I could at least hear it hit, and then after I heard nothing for what seemed a long time, finally Pemberton said, "I felt something."

"You're not ten or fifteen feet down, dude. I don't know how deep this thing is, but we dropped a chem light. Couldn't see it."

"I thought up was in front of me." Pemberton's voice was faint but I could tell he was now getting a bit upset. Not knowing how far down he was I thought that literally not knowing which way was up had to be freaky.

"I don't think up is where you think it is. Look around a bit."

"Okay. I see it. A little pinprick of light. That's got to be it."

Still trying to remain calm, I said, even though I was thinking the exact opposite, "That's good."

"I'm in cold water. My leg hurts. It's killing, actually."

A few seconds later, I could hear him screaming; the reality of it all must have hit him. "It's freakin' cold as hell down here."

I wanted to keep his mind off things so I said, "You must not be anywhere near hell if it's cold."

"Bite me."

Sounds of him thrashing around, splashing water, and his moans reached us. I looked at Trambley and both of us shrugged our shoulders.

"Do you have your weapon?" I asked, just trying to keep Pemberton talking.

"No. Dropped it. Can't find it in the water."

"Are you swimming?"

"Yeah. Treading water. I'm afloat."

"Do you have your body armor on?" I was trying to think if it would help him float or weigh him down.

He must have read my mind. "It's keeping me warm. It's helping me float."

I thought that he was delusional. I figured all that added weight would have the opposite effect.

"Do you have any weapons?"

"My pistol. Probably doesn't work. Why?"

I was worried that he might have a concussion or might lose consciousness so that's why I was peppering him with questions. I didn't want to irritate him, but I could tell that that was what I was doing.

I looked around. Trambley had taken off to retrieve the rope. I had no idea how heavy those things were, but it was inches thick. I saw him outlined against the night sky as he crested one of those deep ditches and then dropped down again, disappearing from sight. He was putting in an enormous effort. I kept covering him, worried that someone was going to take a crack at him. I kept up a conversation with Mike while keeping an eye on Trambley. He'd begun to slow, and I was torn. I didn't want to leave Pemberton, fearing that if he passed out in that water he could drown. I didn't know what hypothermia could do to someone or what its symptoms were, and it was hard to believe that somebody in the middle of Afghanistan in July could be freezing. Sure, it was cold at night, and all, but how the hell could all of this weird stuff be going on?

I knew that Trambley was busting his ass, and I wanted to help him, but then I noticed that he was now making no real progress at all.

"Drop it. Just get back here," I said to him. Even if he got the rope over to us, I didn't know how much it was going to help. Was either of us capable of going down there and helping Pemberton back out?

Trambley came back gassed and upset with himself and the situation. Still, he said, "I can't do it. The frickin' thing's too heavy. I need help or we've got to get some other guys here . . ." His voice trailed off.

The other elements of the platoon were conducting the

operation, keeping radio silence as best they could. I agreed with Trambley. We needed somebody else to help us out. Trambley took off, not wanting to use the comms to just call in some support. He kept in contact with me, but only when he got to the rally point did he advise the others of what was really going on with our man being down.

I didn't hear what I wanted. "No go, Irv. We're about to hit the objective."

"Roger that."

I knew we needed to do something, so I contacted Casey. "Sergeant, Pemberton's down there quite a ways. I'd have to say forty to fifty feet."

"We'll get CSAR out here then."

I'd seen a Discovery Channel special once about the Combat Search and Rescue units. I never thought I'd see them in person. Mostly, the air force used them to get downed pilots back. I wondered if anybody anywhere in the military had any kind of experience rescuing a guy from a hole in the ground. This was the kind of thing a miner might have to do.

I knew that the only thing I needed to do at that point was stick close to Pemberton as best I could. I hunkered down, lying on my side straddling the edge of the concrete and the hole.

"Irv? I'm hearing lots of stuff down here."

I thought of the fighting tunnels I'd read so much about as a kid. What if during all those years of fighting with the

Soviets the Afghan fighters had done the same thing? It seemed plausible. Why would there be a forty- to fifty-foot-deep hole in the middle of this field outside a village?

I knew it could sound bad, but I said to Mike, "If I hear you screaming and anybody else is down there with you, I'm going to pump all twenty rounds down there."

Nobody wanted to be held captive. We knew what the Taliban and the insurgents in Iraq did to American prisoners, regular military or contract workers. Like IEDs and other aspects of this fighting, we didn't talk about them much, but we all understood one another.

"Okay, man. That's cool. I'm really scared right now. I'm freaking out."

"No worries, dude, I'm here. I've got you covered."

I had images in my mind of some guy screaming something in Pashto and me stepping up and firing into that hole and hearing all those screams. I knew that was what Mike would want me to do, and I knew that if the situation was reversed that was what I'd want him to do. I had asked Mike about his pistol both because I wondered if he'd be able to defend himself or do what he needed to do to not get captured. I knew that I wouldn't be trying to kill him, just firing those rounds down there to take out the bad guys. I knew he'd be good with however that turned out.

The beating sound of a Chinook's rotors made me feel better, knowing that I wouldn't have to be fully responsible for getting Pemberton out of there. That feeling didn't last very long. In order to find us, they needed to shine their IR (infrared) floodlight to illuminate the area. I still had on my night vision, so I couldn't see the large beams pooling on the ground. I was lying next to an enormous hole, much, much larger than I had imagined, and much deeper. I was two feet away from its edge, and I tried to crawl away from it. I put my rifle under my stomach and sprawled out once I felt the rotor wash pushing me. I dug my nails deep into the dirt and tried to dig my toes in as well, but I could feel myself sliding closer and closer to that hole.

I thought I was going to die. I thought that that wind was going to lift my 165-pound body up and deposit it down there near Pemberton. I figured the pilot couldn't see me, and I was also worried about where that helicopter was going to set down. Earlier, we'd been told they couldn't and now here was somebody about to give it a shot. As I looked over my shoulder from my position on my belly, the however-many-ton Chinook was about to land either on top of me or go crashing into that hole and on top of Pemberton. They hovered about twenty feet above me and then began inching closer and closer toward me.

I lay there wondering how this was all going to end, when I saw the black belly of that bird start to rise again. As soon as it was clear enough for me to stand, I scrambled to my feet and ran and slid down the slight embankment of the ditch. From that position, I could see something being lowered from the Chinook. A moment later, it receded back into the cargo area. A moment after that, the Chinook spun around and retreated.

"Irv. What the hell is going on?"

Pemberton's desperation tore at me.

"They're coming back. Don't worry. They'll be here again," I told him, expressing my hope rather than anything I knew to be true.

I contacted our platoon leader, hoping he'd know what was going on.

"The rig wasn't long enough," he said. "They brought a forty-footer but said it wasn't near long enough."

I couldn't believe my estimate had been so bad. How far down was Pemberton? Had he slid or had he fallen all the way to the bottom?

"We need you here. You've got to cover for us before we go in."

"Roger that."

Orders are orders, but I hated the thought of leaving Pemberton there. He seemed to have gotten worse. When I was talking to him, he'd allow a long time before responding, and more and more he was saying things that had nothing to do with what I'd asked him, talking about his car and making other random observations. I wasn't sure how badly he was hurt, how the water was impacting his situation, and just how long it was going to take for the CSAR guys to finally get to him. I had to refocus though. As I gathered my gear and rekitted, I looked at the wristband I wore. I consulted the maps I kept there like a quarterback consulting his playlist.

Before I set out, I stood at the edge of the hole and shouted down, "Mike, I've got go, buddy. You're good. They're coming right back. They've got you."

I didn't want to wait for a response. I figured that if I got out of there, I could tell myself that I hadn't heard him, that he was still awake and doing okay.

When I got to the rally point I had to answer a bunch of questions that I didn't want to. Guys were wondering what had happened; some wanted to know what hole I was talking about, how only one guy out of all of us could have fallen in there, how lucky we were that it was only one of us, and more and more things that had nothing to do with what I was concerned about. I didn't blame the guys, but I just wanted to get on with taking on this objective and get the hell out of there so I could see how Mike was doing.

We set up for an explosive breach to get the door open. I was in position and watching through my sights as they put the C-4 charge in place. My mind was on Mike, but I kept my eyes on the windows, making sure the rooms were clear. Before I knew it, the doors blew open, the flash bangs popped, and out of the smoke and noise two of the guys were leading out the target. As they were doing all that, I spotted a tall building that I knew I'd have to free-climb since Pemberton had the ladder. It gave me a vantage point to overlook almost the entire area, including Pemberton's location.

With the guy in hand and the area clear, I made my way onto that roof. I looked back toward Pemberton's position, hoping I could see the progress the CSAR guys were making. The helicopter was coming in and I listened to the live reports over the radios. I turned back away, listening to the action, while overwatching the area with my rifle and making sure to mission focus. A lot of people in the village had come out after all the commotion went down. I lit each of them up with my laser, got a distance on them. I sensed that none of them were hostiles, just a bunch of onlookers. I saw no weapons, no sign of an immediate threat. Being able to spot a potential hostile was an important part of our training. Evaluating a person's demeanor, watching their eye movements, what they did with their hands and bodies, had all become second nature out there.

I turned back to Pemberton. He'd been extracted, wrapped in heat blankets, but the report wasn't good. He was in shock, hypothermia had him, and they'd do other evaluations, but for right now they just needed to get him warm. They estimated that he'd fallen some seventy-five to eighty feet. They were sending a diver down to retrieve any sensitive items—his weapon, his laser, and a few other items. Later the diver would say that he'd gone down an additional forty feet below the water and still hadn't contacted the bottom. At that point, he had to stop his search. No one had any idea how far down that hole went.

As I was on that roof, I heard the muffled sound of a suppressed shot. Perkins and his sniper element had fired on a secondary objective a few hundred meters from our position. Perkins observed a man coming out of his house with an AK-47, and he was headed in the direction of a secondary assault force. He had to take the guy out and he did. I scrambled off the roof and over to that position. Everything was secure, so I headed back toward Pemberton.

The Chinook was hovering about a hundred meters offset from the hole. The ramp was lowered and was balanced on top of that ledge we'd been walking across. The helicopter was angled nose up and the ramp was at about a thirty-degree angle. I knew what the plan was, but I couldn't believe that these air force guys were going to do it. They had Pemberton on a stretcher, and they were running along at a pretty good pace. Instead of taking that balance beam, they were moving up and down through those ditches and mounds. They were running up and down that roller coaster, one of them in his wet suit and mask. I was impressed. I knew that those CSAR guys had a serious adrenaline overload happening. They didn't get to have boots on the ground that often. They got to the Chinook and up the ramp they went with Pemberton, handing him off to the crew chiefs and medics who were waiting. A few moments later, they were in the air.

The whole unit was back together near the hole, and of course, the conversation was all about what had happened and how. I knew that Pemberton was going to be okay. He was in great hands and every report said that his vital signs were strong.

We decided that the hole was pretty damn dangerous and we didn't want to have to deal again with anything like what we'd just gone through. The consensus was that it needed to be blown up. I had no idea how they were going to do it, but I knew what my role had to be. I positioned myself about two hundred meters from the hole and scanned the area, ready to take out anybody who approached. With all the noise we were about to make, I knew that those curious folks were going to get even more curious. I hoped the explosion would discourage them from coming to check things out.

We decided that if we all contributed our hand grenades and tossed them in, that would take care of the hole. Ten guys stood in a semicircle with their grenades. They pulled the pins and dropped the grenades in. Six seconds later a muffled explosive sound came up out of the hole, and some smoke drifted up after that.

"That was stupid."

"What the hell."

"There ain't enough grenades in the province."

We didn't know what was at the bottom of that pit. For all we knew it could have been paved or there was concrete down there. Our grenades could have just made the hole deeper, and if there was a system of tunnels, then the whole area could have collapsed like a giant sinkhole. I knew that I didn't want to be near it with those explosions going off.

Eventually, we got some mortar rounds and an AC-130 dropped a high-explosive 105 howitzer round in there. With all those mortar rounds going off, we figured we'd have to see something happen. Nothing. A guy tossed in a thermobaric grenade. Nothing. Thermobarics are really devastating, and I've seen a whole house brought down by one of them. A bunch of fine dirt started falling like snow. Smoke trailed out of that chimneylike hole. I was keeping my distance. No way I was going near there. What if my fear of heights kicked in? Vertigo? Anything.

Finally after all the smoke cleared, everyone agreed that nothing was going to put a dent in that hole, let alone cover it up. Still, we were like guys everywhere. We couldn't believe that something that simple could be defeating our best efforts and our equipment. A few more howitzer rounds got dropped, but the Pemberton hole would not be defeated.

At that point, after the last of those howitzer rounds had cleared, the Chinooks came back in to extract us. When we got back to the airfield, I saw a few of the CSAR guys sitting around on a pickup truck. They waved me over, and I sat on the tailgate.

"How the hell is that guy still alive?" one of them asked.

"I have no idea. What do you mean?"

"I went down in there," another of them said. "There's no way he scraped the sides of that hole. He fell straight down into that thing. I was eighty feet down. I saw him and he was conscious. He was doing little flutter kicks and other stuff to stay afloat. How long was he down there?"

I shrugged and said, "I don't know exactly, a couple of hours."

"Freakin' amazing."

"What was weird," one of Pemberton's rescuers said, "was that there was an old ladder down there. A wood ladder floating around. He said he hit that. That was what fractured his tibia."

"That's all that happened?" I asked. "A busted bone in his leg?"

"He hit his head on a rock. His helmet stayed on though. Good thing. He said other stuff kept falling on him."

We all laughed.

"He said it was ten feet. Fifteen feet."

"And you're a sniper? Can't judge distance without a scope?"

"Not without depth perception and night visit. "I said, and we all laughed.

I had to admit it all seemed ridiculous. Pemberton and I had walked away without a scratch from a twenty-four-hour firefight and had escaped from a deadly sniper, and now he was seriously injured walking on an operation that, otherwise, went off without a hitch.

I kept thinking about that helmet and asked what happened to it. No one knew but they said that based on how it looked, it wasn't going to do anybody any good anymore. The conversation went on with these air force guys echoing what we'd all been saying. This was the most bizarre thing we'd seen. None of us could figure out what the purpose of that hole was. The diver guessed that it went down for another sixty to eighty feet. All I could think of was a missile silo or something, but even that made no sense at all. Thank goodness it wasn't a dry hole.

I wanted to see Pemberton, so one of the drivers took me over to a hospital in Kandahar to see him. When I walked into his room, Mike was sitting up, propped up by pillows. He had a huge grin on his face.

"I'm so sorry, man," he said.

"What? Are you kidding me?"

"I missed out. I wasn't there to back you up."

"Forget about that. You just survived a HALO jump into the center of the earth. You're a superhero. Holeman or something."

"It was freaking scary, Irv."

He described what it was like, telling me how as he was falling, he twisted in the air and lost his rifle, but he unholstered his pistol on the way down.

"Are you kidding me? You told me you were only down there ten or fifteen feet."

"Didn't matter. I thought I'd stepped through a doorway. All you guys ahead of me had disappeared in the dark and I figured you'd gone through a doorway. I thought maybe I'd tripped and I was going into the middle of a courtyard, and I'd need my weapon. Guys were coming after me."

"You were tripping all right." I wasn't sure how much of this was what Pemberton really remembered, the effects of his knock on the head, or if it was the drugs they'd given him for the pain.

"You mean you had the presence of mind, as you were falling," I continued, "to take out your weapon and aim?"

"Yes."

"Did you not feel or hear the wind whistling past your ears?"

"I didn't feel any wind. None at all. I didn't feel anything as I was falling. I was weightless."

"What happened when you hit?"

"Felt nothing at all. I was like a sack of shit. I must have been all loose." He paused for a second. "I don't remember much, but I think that my leg hit first." He screwed his face up in pain.

"You okay?"

He shrugged. "I have no idea. Everything just seems so strange right now."

"The water?"

"Yeah, I think maybe that snapped me out of it. I don't remember hitting my head, but they told me about my helmet. Maybe I was out. I remember trying to stay afloat, kicking every once in a while."

Everything had worked out perfectly for him. The cold water had numbed him so that his leg pain wasn't so bad that he couldn't move it. He remembered holding on to that ladder with one hand, the pistol in the other, and using his arm to tread water a bit.

"The worst thing was how dark it was. I couldn't see a thing. That freaked me out. Until that PJ came down to get me I felt so alone."

"You couldn't hear me?"

"I could. But there was this weird echo. I knew it was you and I understood some of what you were saying."

I thought about how lucky we both were that I'd taken out my hearing protection. Normally, I waited until I'd reached the objective before doing that.

As I was sitting there considering that, Sergeant Casey came in. He had this superserious look on his face, and was walking with hands behind him. He stopped at the edge of the bed, on the opposite side of where I was standing.

"Michael Pemberton." He produced a sheet of folded paper from behind him and set it down on Pemberton's lap.

All was quiet while Mike unfolded it. A second later Pemberton started laughing. He set it down again, and I could see a Navy SEAL trident on the top of the paper,

like it was official letterhead. It offered the congratulations
of the entire SEAL team community, and he was awarded
his fake SEAL trident and HALO wings. He'd just had
the free fall and swim of his life, so it all seemed appropri-
ate.

"Yeah. I'm just glad I was in the navy." Mike had done
six years of service with them before joining us.

I added that to my list of—call it what you want—
coincidence, providence, whatever, that surrounded this man
down situation.

A couple of days later, Pemberton was released from the
hospital. I went to get him and he was in a wheelchair.

"Can you believe it? A frickin' rolling cage. Like a circus
animal on parade."

I thought maybe he was kidding, but he wasn't smiling.

"This sucks. I want to stay here with you guys, Irv."

"I know. Don't worry about it. I'd rather see you go home.
We've only got a month left."

I didn't have to add anything more about how short time
was stress time.

"Besides, you'd gotten a whole lot of kills. I'm the Reaper,
remember." By that point, his kill count was fourteen. He
was damn good with that Win Mag.

We talked for a while longer, both of us knowing the
complicated truth that we both wanted him to go and
wanted him to stay, just like I wanted out of there and wanted
to stick around. I also told him that as soon as he got back

to the States I was going to be in touch. Finally I added, "But seriously, if you don't want to go, I'll take your place."

He laughed and then reached over and pulled me into a hug.

"I'll see you when you're back," he told me.

We received status updates on each of his flights when he e-mailed us while waiting for the next one to take off. Every time I responded by asking him if he'd gone down in any holes.

He kept telling me to be safe, and I think that now that he was out of the bubble, no longer under the influence of our collective disassociation with the very real possibilities we faced, I could sense that he was upset. That was especially true once he finally got back to Benning.

For so long, we both had been committed to taking care of each other. Now that he could no longer do it, when he spoke the words "take care of yourself," they took on a meaning that neither of us liked.

Of course, we couldn't let that moment linger too long. "Just so you know, the nurse that traveled with me was smoking hot."

Once Mike was back in the States, I called him. The first thing he told me was that he was sitting at home enjoying some good homemade chocolate chip cookies.

"I always knew you'd turn out to be the master of E and E," I told him, finally resorting to tech-speak with him, using the shorthand for evasion and escape, "but I never figured you'd find a hole that would take you all the way back to Georgia."

Through a mouthful of crumbs, he said, "I gotta tell you, it's a whole lot easier indexing targets when they're in a Tupperware bowl, my friend, a whole lot easier."

"Well, you keep enjoying life there on Sesame Street."

"Roger that. This one's for you," he said, as the sounds of another cookie being crammed into his face crackled over the line.

8. Rumble in the Rubble

As much as I was going to miss having Mike around, we all knew that he was—as far as him being a part of sniper team—replaceable. In fact, well before Mike was back home playing Cookie Monster, I was paired with another sniper. Brent had been working out of Camp Bastion and flew in two days after what I had named in my mind the "Longest Day." I was just coming out of my hibernation, when I received word that he was arriving. I knew Brent by reputation. He'd been in the sniper platoon for a while, and the funny thing was, any time we got a new guy coming in, it was cause for a kind of celebration. We were glad to touch base with somebody from outside the group we'd been deployed with. They could fill us in on news of the rest of the platoon, let us know that everybody, hopefully, was okay. If not, then at least we'd know what to expect when we got back home.

The army had its own way of setting up sniper teams. Frequently, the spotter was a guy who was senior to the shooter. That was the case with Brent. I wasn't sure how old he was, but rumor had it that he'd been around in the sniper section for quite a while. He was a really good competitive shooter, and I'd heard that he'd won a few of them, and competed in the International Sniper Competition held at Fort Benning. As its name says, the ISC includes snipers from different parts of the world as well as the U.S. military. Civilian teams, and police Special Tactics and Weapons, also compete.

When I was in sniper school there, I'd heard about the event, but hadn't participated in it. (Eventually, in 2009, I competed shortly after returning Stateside and placed in the top five.) I thought it was cool that for basically seventy-two hours straight this competition went on with stalking, urban shooting and orienteering, and what was called "shooting under stressful conditions." Now that I'd been downrange and operational as a sniper, and I'd been doing these things for real, the idea of a competition didn't quite have the same mystique that it once did. That doesn't mean that I didn't have any respect for the guys who competed in them. It was all about honing your skills and preparing yourself for the real thing and there was a whole lot of pride at stake. Whether it was guys from the Tenth Mountain Division, the Third Infantry Division, or especially the marines' Scout Sniper School, or one of the international SWAT teams, bragging rights were on the line.

As soon as I saw Brent come into our compound I had a

better recollection of who he was. Brent was a smaller guy like me, only five five or five six, but he packed a lot more muscle on that small frame. He looked like a wrestler or a football player, with his thick neck and torso. He was so ripped that his arms didn't fall naturally to his sides, but stuck out a bit. He had a big old grin on his face, too. That's when I remembered a few of the pranks he'd pulled on guys over time. He was into shaving cream and loved hitting guys in the face with "whipped cream" pies as a way of honoring them when they'd received some kind of citation or otherwise done well. He was also pretty good at imitating people's voices, and more than one guy in the sniper section got all worked up by a voice mail message from one of our "commanders" who'd asked to see us immediately.

Brent was from New Jersey and I was disappointed that he didn't have that wise-guy fuggedaboutit accent. We met in the TOC and he walked in with his stout shoulders loaded with bags. He set them down and shook my hand.

"Sergeant Irving," he said, sounding like a butler out of an English movie. He cleared his throat and then said in his normal voice, "Hey, Irv. Or should I say Reaper? Or is it Mr. Reaper?"

The English accent was a reminder that he'd been at Bastion, a British military base that was right next to our marines' Camp Leatherneck. Neither of us could have known this then, but Britain's Prince Harry would one day be stationed at Bastion.

We talked for a bit, catching up on some of the guys and what we'd both been up to.

"I'd heard you guys were getting some, but I thought some of it was just—" He stopped and shrugged. "You know."

"No. It's been for real."

"Nice. That's what I was hoping to hear. Can't believe I haven't had any trigger time. Unless you count those street-lights and stuff."

Brent had been deployed multiple times and he'd yet to fire on a human target. That just pointed out again how unusual my experience had been, how much trigger time Pemberton and I had had in so short a period. We were just six weeks shy of ending our hundred-plus-days rotation in country, and Pemberton had left with fourteen confirmed kills. When I told Brent that, he tipped back in his chair and whistled. "H-o-l-y s-h-i-t," he said.

"And what about you?"

"Twenty six."

"Wow. A dozen more."

That led to a discussion about how Mike and I had been operating and that I didn't believe that the by-the-books sniper/shooter relationship really worked given the specifics of our operations. He needed to do more than just select targets and assist in aiming and all of that. It would have been even weirder for me to have Brent be that kind of caddy for me when he already had so many years in the section.

"You tell me what you want, and I'm there," he said. He bent down and unlocked one of his hard cases. Inside was a .50 caliber Barrett with Leupold Mark 4 scope. The M82 was, and is, the only semiautomatic .50 cal in the world. It was a great SASR (special application scoped rifle), but I told him it was one that he'd probably want to leave at home when we went out. The same was true for his Win Mag. Fortunately, he was an SR-25 guy.

While I was giving him the rundown on what we'd been doing and what we found effective in terms of appearance of objects and the different measurements of things in our area of operation, how the enemy was responding to contact, Sergeant Peters joined us.

Brent and Peters shook hands. No sooner had Peters told him that he hoped he was ready for a good four to six weeks, all our pagers went off. It was interesting to see how different Brent's response was to ours. His eyes lit up. I knew better than to be too excited. Things had had a way of evolving that didn't always play out the way we'd planned. I still had visions of Pemberton dropping down into that hole. For that reason, and a few others, I was glad that we weren't going to be heading out toward Marjah or any of the other more rural areas. Our objective was right in the middle of Kandahar itself.

I felt more comfortable in the urban environment than I did out in the country. We had encountered much less contact in Kandahar than anywhere else. I didn't know if it was because the coalition forces were a much more obvious and larger presence in the city, but I guess that was true. The Taliban had, for the most part, fled the city. That made sense. Why would they stay where they had the greatest chance of being tracked down? It also seemed like the people in Kandahar, the Afghan civilians, were more likely to provide us with human intel on these guys. It was easier for informants to be anonymous in the city, and in terms of sheer numbers, you had more people and therefore a greater chance of finding someone willing to cooperate with us. In the small villages, those residents had no place to go, really. If the Taliban found out you'd ratted them out, they could easily track you down.

It was hard for me to understand the mentality of the Afghan people. I didn't really try to figure them out, but there were times when I was really surprised at their behavior. I had to get it out of my head that they were like us. I don't mean that in terms of culture or religion, but there were times when I was thinking about how my family, friends, neighbors, and I myself would have reacted if some foreign military were in the area and conducting the kinds of operations we were.

It seemed strange to me that you could get so used to combat operations being conducted nearby that you'd be able to sleep while huge helicopters thundered overhead. I knew that we landed a safe distance from our objectives, but I kept thinking that the sound of our arrival must have carried to the location where our targets were. I don't know if they understood what kind of surveillance they were under, or if the Taliban members we were after knew that they'd be tracked if they ran, but I still thought it strange that we could arrest and neutralize so many of our targets right in the buildings. I knew that they weren't a regular army so to speak, but why weren't there defensive perimeters, guards and watches? I knew that it was an unfair assumption to make, but especially out in the middle of nowhere, which seemed to be most places, it seemed like we were dealing with people who had a limited understanding of what was really going on in what we all knew to be a war on terror.

Since I'd never been through anything like what they'd experienced, it was hard to imagine what it would be like to go through your day-to-day routine while a war was going on in your country, in your village, in a house in a nearby compound. I knew some people who lived in D.C. and in New York, and immediately after the attacks on the Pentagon and World Trade Center, there was a military presence around. They talked about how weird it was to see men in uniform with weapons on them patrolling around. That didn't last for very long, but they said that they still never got used to the sight of someone standing there in the place they lived with a rifle slung across their chest. Maybe over time they would have adjusted to it, it would have blended into the background, just like the rest of the guys and I got used to moving around and among the Afghan people.

I'd been in Baghdad, Tikrit, and Mosul, so I knew what it was like to be on operations in the middle of a city's commotion. Even though they were all undertaken at night, there was still a fair amount of street activity. But when you were operating in the rural areas where a few mopeds or people on bikes was the extent of the traffic, it felt weird to be out there. I knew that at night most people were asleep, so it made sense that not a whole lot of activity was going on, but it seemed more dreamlike, like something out of a postapocalypse movie.

In the city, things felt more real, more familiar, and that, combined with encountering less enemy contact, made it seem safer.

That wasn't true, however, for this first operation with Brent as my partner. That had nothing to do with him. He clearly had a lot of experience, and before we gave a full brief, I said to him, "Hey, do you want to do this? Do you want command of the element?"

"Thanks. No. I'm in your territory. I have no real idea how you guys like to do things."

"We can adapt. We're flexible."

"Whatever you're doing seems to be working. Keep at it."

I was glad that the mission seemed relatively routine and would be in an area where we might encounter only light contact if any at all. I knew what Brent was going through. He'd just come in, hadn't gotten settled at all, and now he was planning to go out with us. I'd been in his shoes just a month and a half earlier. Our target was the head of a suicide-bomb cell. It was impossible for me to imagine how someone could recruit me to do what these bombers did. I know that I'd signed up for a dangerous duty, and I was willing to die for my country, but there was nothing as absolute as the certainty of death these men and women faced. The people who did the recruiting and training, the individuals who sourced the bomb-making materials and then built them, were about as despicable as it gets.

IEDs were one thing on my mind. As much as they were part of a tactic we all hated, in some ways, they were a part of war. I didn't see suicide bombers in the same way, mostly because the most frequent targets were civilians. The army eventually released a study that said there were 106 suicide-bombing attacks in Afghanistan in 2009, the year of this deployment, and that the chances of one inflicting casualties on NATO troops was very low. It would take more than three suicide bombers to cause harm to one member of the international force. That was good news, but not for the civilian population. Hundreds of people were dying in attacks that were coming on average once every three days. The attacks were of two kinds—explosives strapped to a person or a bomb placed in a vehicle that a terrorist drove.

With the population and vehicle density being greater in

the city, it made sense that we had to be even more vigilant while moving around. Whenever we went on one of these types of missions, I was always more on edge. As the sniper team leader, I was responsible for selecting tactical positions for my guys. That meant I could be the one who put them in the wrong place at the wrong time. Also, if we were going after one of these commanders, and they were involved with explosives, it stood to reason that explosives were going to be nearby. Putting ourselves in proximity to those materials heightened the risk. For the most part, the sniper team was a fairly good distance away from the targeted objective. I wanted to get the best shots at them or any other enemy that needed to be taken down, and that generally meant not being danger close to any explosives that might get detonated.

That wasn't as true in the confines of the city. For this operation, we would be operating in a location about a mile or so from the Presidential Palace, the Ministry of Education, and several shopping centers and theaters. We were going to be almost exclusively operating at night, so there wouldn't be a lot of people on the streets, if any at all, but with all those multistory buildings, we faced multiple points from which enemy fire might come.

Every sniper has his own preferences on gear, and though Pemberton and I didn't agree on choice of weapons, we basically kitted ourselves in the same way. Brent came out, after having stashed his things in Pemberton's old room, wearing his hard-plate in a Molle carrier. The Molle kit was very useful for the assaulters because it had many attachment points on it from which you could place items— flash bangs, grenades, multiple pouches, et cetera. Having all that extra equipment strapped to the front of that carrier made it easier to get snagged on a ladder's steps and made lying prone for hours on end torturous. That's why I went with the soft-plate carrier with a hard-plate inside it. I liked how the soft-plate conformed to my body, so I'd remove the softer material or plates, and replace them with the hard-plate that was stout enough to stop the 7.62 by 39 mm (used in the AK-47) the enemy used. I'd also put some cardboard in there and tape it all up to make up for the difference in thickness between the two kinds of material.

I felt a lot more streamlined that way and, for me, being comfortable and having maximum flexibility was important. The downside was that I couldn't attach much other gear to it and especially not a pistol. That didn't matter to me. Unlike Brent, who wanted his pistol front and center and within easy reach on his chest, I didn't have much use for a sidearm. To that point in my deployment, I hadn't had any use at all for one. Climbing up a building, you want to have your pistol at the ready in case you have to fire on the way up or once on top of the roof. To that point, I had met zero resistance while climbing or mounting a building.

The two of us eyed each other, not saying anything, but you could tell we were both assessing. We didn't look like a team. Imagine two football players of the same size and one is wearing the type of shoulder pads that a lineman might use and the other wearing what a wide receiver does. Pemberton and I had been through a couple of sniper schools together and had been in Afghanistan for six weeks, and we'd hashed out all the details of our kit and our approach already. We were truly a team and looked it. I didn't want to make any judgments about Brent's ability based on his gear, but I did have some concern about how he was going to be able to maneuver quickly and easily over and around all the obstacles we were likely to encounter.

On the one hand, I knew that this was just a case of our appearances being different, but it served as a reminder that we were going to war together for the first time and that the kind of things that I took for granted with Pemberton weren't going to be as easily understood and communicated with Brent. It was like Troy Aikman losing a guy like Michael Irvin and having to adjust to a Kelvin Martin-type guy. Both pros. Both great at what they do, but different in the sense of each knowing exactly what the other is going to do and where they're going to be when a play gets busted or hasn't developed yet.

Add up all these factors, and I was little bit uneasy, but a good uneasy, wanting to be extra vigilant. After we landed at a compound the Brits operated out of, some of that uneasiness grew stronger. We're all creatures of habit, and this was a new experience for me, landing at someone else's compound and then immediately going straight outside of the wire and into a crowded urban environment.

At least I could count on one thing. Wade Rice was part of my team, out in front with three other guys. Wade wanted to be a sniper very badly, so he was always eager to be attached to my sniper team and he frequently volunteered to carry my extra ammo, ladder, and things like that. He wasn't being a suck-up or anything like that, he was just a really good teammate who was willing to lend a hand. Often, he'd go out with us and tail behind me and observe how we conducted ourselves during the operation. Behind me was Brent, and behind him, the rest of our small element.

As I was walking along, I remembered something Pemberton had said to me. "Where there's people there's shit. Where there's lots of people, there's lots of shit."

We'd been operating out in the boonies exclusively, so I'd forgotten about the assault our senses would undertake. The smell of human feces, decaying flesh—I saw bodies of dogs in the ditches that ran on each side of the roads we patrolled along—was strong and I fought down my gag reflex.

The streets were empty, and the windows of a few homes were illuminated. Overhead, a rat's nest of wires conducted the intermittent flow of electric current. Ahead of me, I'd see a light come on, flicker, die, and then revive. The wires were low enough that if you weren't careful and carried your muzzle too high you could end up frying yourself. I felt comfortable having Bruno and Sergeant Val in front of us. We were about five hundred meters from our objective when we spotted a small structure on the ground, or at least from a distance it looked like a structure. A pile of rocks, maybe eight or nine feet high, a random pile of junk really, sat offset to the left of the center of the intersection we'd arrived at.

The lead was skirting around it, including Bruno and Sergeant Val, but the K9 hadn't shown any signs of a detection. The guys in front had their weapons pointed at that pile as they made their tactical evasion. I halted my guys and we backed off a bit before spreading out. As the point guys approached, a bright white light passed by the head of one of the guys out front. They all immediately dropped to the ground, and then I heard a loud crack and its echoing report move through the streets.

With a few of the streetlights on, our night vision PVS-14 and 15 goggles were flaring out as the artificial light polluted the area, and for me, that lessened the feeling of a possible threat. We hadn't received any intel about the possibility of a sniper attack. Until we'd gotten to that object in the street, everything had been proceeding so smoothly. I was now in a here-we-go-again mind-set. The lead group began taking fire and returning it, killing a couple of hostiles. Brent and I dropped down in the prone position, right in the middle of the street, in order to get a good visual on the enemy. Some of the guys in the element went to the sides of the narrow street. None of us wanted to get into those ditches if we could help it. Brent and I lay there scanning, getting a fix on the enemy, focusing in on their faces and heads.

I could see bullets passing over the heads of the guys in front of us, and then felt them going over our heads, dropping short of the rest of the guys, who were about twenty meters to our rear directly at our six. Finally, I could see where the shots were coming from—directly ahead of us and down our intended path of travel. That sucked. No one behind Brent and me could get off a shot. They had to be concerned about our position, whether or not we were going to stay at our level, stand up, or whatever. That meant they couldn't safely fire over our heads. It would be too dangerous to just open up with an M4 or MK-48 machine gun over our heads as well as that of the lead element in front of us. Wade Rice had been able to lay down a few rounds of suppressive fire, but it was now down to him and the rest of us to get some precise rounds on target.

The fire got really intense as I zoomed in on my scope.

"Brent. We got targets right behind that pile. I see heads popping up around it."

"Roger. Got it."

I could hear the excitement in his voice. I watched him for a second getting situated. As excited as we were and that being Brent's first time firing on a live target, we all kept in mind that smooth is fast in any situation. I couldn't fault him though, he'd been itching for some trigger time, and now it was happening. I turned my attention back to the pile. At first, all I saw was heads peeking around it briefly. Then I saw one of the enemy lean out, at nearly a ninety-degree angle from the pile. He had his AK out away from his body and he was just spraying and praying. Watching the tip of his muzzle spark, I focused on the center of his head. I didn't have time to dial the elevation down, so I simply held low using the mil dot reticle. His head exploded, spraying brain matter on the structure in front of him and his AK became a baton as it pinwheeled briefly.

A second later, and for no good reason that I can think of, a second target stood up and started yelling. Whether he was scared by the sight of his buddy going down or if he just had that suicide mentality, it didn't really matter. I heard a shot ring out of a Knight's Armament suppressor and watched the guy fall. I could hear the faint excitement in Brent's voice as he yelled, "I got him." I guess after that many years of training to precisely kill another man, your brain is already used to the sensation. I knew that getting him wasn't the end to our night. The guys in front were still basically pinned down. They could fire, but it was ineffective because they were in a prone position and so close to the enemy position.

Out of the corner of my eye, I caught sight of something

approaching from the left. A white pickup truck came into view, and I immediately flashed on the reports we'd been hearing about suicide bombers and vehicles. An instant later that thought was gone. Mounted to the back of the pickup—I could see now that it was a Toyota Hilux—was a DShK machine gun. I heard a series of loud thudding sounds and watched as the guys in front of my position rolled to the side of the road and down into the sewage trench. The guy operating the weapon turned to pivot the gun, but the driver was going so fast (I'd say about thirty-five to fifty miles an hour), he could only direct his fire down the right side of the road. In a second or two, the vehicle had passed through the intersection.

We were all on comms telling everybody to take cover. We knew that weapon was designed to take out tanks and that none of us—no matter if we were hard-plate, soft-plate, or whatever combination of plate—would survive getting struck by one of those giant rounds. We were fortunate the driver had flown through that shooting lane, but that gave the guys behind the pile of rubble an opportunity to key in on us. Brent and I rose from our position and I jumped into the trench, feeling its liquid and chunky ooze all along my lower legs up to my thighs. I had to fight off thoughts of what the hell I'd just jumped into and focus on taking out those guys. I would have jumped into just about anything, including a raging inferno, to escape the devastation that DShK could hand out.

At this point, the six of us were in a pretty tight little cluster. Brent was crouching up against the side wall. I don't know if he was braver than the rest of us or just didn't want to get into the shit-ooze, since just the bottoms of his Merrells contacted the slop. Wade had joined me in the trench and we sloshed around, and I kept thinking of the pit toilets at some of the state parks I'd been to. A cloud of mosquitoes and other flying insects rose up, clogging my nose and marring my vision. I thought of swatting at them, but I'd gotten some of the slop on one hand.

"Hey, Irv," I heard Wade scream out, "I hope you took your dox pills."

Everybody knew that I didn't like taking the antimalarials and other drugs. I hated the idea of taking all the stuff we were handed out, especially since one of them had made me sick as a dog. I knew that I was supposed to take it with food, so I swallowed it and followed that up with a can of ravioli that my folks had sent me. About ten minutes later, I didn't even make it to the Porta-Johns before I puked up that ravioli. The guys got a big laugh of that, telling me that I needed to chew my food, since that pile looked exactly the same as it had coming out of the can.

I don't know why Rice chose that moment to remind me of that. I was trying to get eyes on the guys behind the rubble pile. Since Rice had the most effective weapon for this kind of job, I motioned for him to advance in front of Brent and me. Brent was at my six, and just as we were sighting on a couple of targets, we heard the truck's engine revving and its tires squealing as it came back from our right this time. Fortunately, for some reason, he was focused on the right side of the street, and we were all on the left in the trench.

The intersection was fairly well lit, which was bad for us, but it did allow me to see the gunner's eyes. He spotted us, but he'd advanced too far to get the weapon trained on us. I knew that they'd come around again, and hoped that they wouldn't do something smart like circle to our rear and come up the road parallel to our position. The guys on point were still taking heavy fire; bullets skipped off the pavement, like deadly stones skipped across a pond, rising to head height. Still, they kept returning fire, while I kept thinking about the longest day when Pemberton and I and the rest of our recon element had been pinned down for so long. I felt bad for those guys, but because of what I'd just been through, and how close we all came to getting wiped out, I wasn't about to put on my Superman cape and do anything foolishly heroic. I knew what the result would be and I wouldn't benefit anybody's chances of getting out of this thing if I went all gung ho and charged.

I don't know if it was because Brent hadn't been through what Pemberton and I had, but he didn't hesitate much at all. He was still standing and firing away. Because of the enemy's concealment, there wasn't much chance of a precise shot, and that was what I was trained and expected to provide. Shooting from low to high wasn't the optimal choice, but it was the only one I had. I'd catch a glimpse of a guy poking out and I'd fire. I was growing frustrated, thinking that the only way to get those guys was with some weapon that could pierce that pile of rubble. I realized that I was wrong about them not establishing a perimeter. It was clear that that rubble was placed very strategically. I wondered for an instant if there were others scattered around that area to protect the suicide squad's commander.

All this time, I'd been counting and I came up with six shooters. I asked Brent what he had and he came with eight. We split the difference and reported in seven. I got on the comms and said that we had the seven enemy shooters and the rubble pile at that location. I wanted a 203 launched on them, but we were danger close and shrapnel could tear us up.

We had to advance, outflank them, and then take them out one at a time. I told Rice and Brent to stay there and keep up the suppressive fire. I was going to rejoin the rest of the third squad to flank off those shooters and be done with it. The one wild card was the damn pickup and machine gun. I could hear its engine again and it sounded as if it was moving at high speed. I looked over at Brent and he was bug-eyed, as I probably was, and we both knew what was about to go down. One round fired into that trench could easily take out him, Rice, and me. The thought, briefly, passed through my mind that we could submerge ourselves completely, but that was one I easily dismissed. If we could compress ourselves and press up against the side of the trench and get as low as possible, we'd be the smallest target we could be.

A moment later, I looked up and Rice was standing up. I could see a tracer round coming in from the DShK, and I swore it was as big as gallon jug of milk flaming toward our heads. Rice reached out and put his M4 on fully automatic, something I'd never seen anyone do and that we were trained not to do, and he opened up with that thing, firing at the pile, emptying out the magazine. Spent casings came cascading out his weapon, looking like they were rolling off some reversed assembly line.

He slid home another magazine, and this time flipped the weapon to semi and started to fire more accurate and better spaced rounds, squeezing one off every second or so. Bullets were still flying over us, but Rice just stood there, shouting, as if this was some Hollywood version of the scene "You mother f---ers are shooting at me!"

We could hear the truck, and the guys behind the pile were firing at him and then the DHsK let loose on us. I couldn't believe what I was seeing and hearing. I thought that Rice had lost it. Maybe he had gotten hit and now he was just jolted with adrenaline and this was one final giant spurt of it coursing through his body. The truck was getting closer, and this time it was coming in head-on. That must have gotten Rice's attention. He did a 360 into the muck with us, his eyes as big as coasters.

We ducked down as low as we could, and the truck screamed past us, maybe ten feet from our position, and I could see a white spot on the sidewall of one of the tires, spinning crazily off center. Their gunner was blazing the trench just above us, the pressure of the bullets firing overhead a kind of fanning hiss and sizzle. I kept thinking that Rice should get up and take out that driver. I figured that now that they knew where we were, all they had to do was swing that truck toward us and either enter the ditch and run us over, or rain down more .50 cal rounds on top of us. Once the truck went by, it started to swerve, and I figured that was it. The driver was trying to slow down and make that U-turn that would end things for us. Rice climbed out of the trench and started firing again, putting rounds into the back of the truck until the sound of the vehicle running into something could be heard over the gunfire.

I was so relieved and I couldn't believe that Rice had taken that truck out all by himself.

Rice stood there shouting, "I got you! I got you!" while pointing and stomping his feet.

I turned my focus to the rubble pile. Out of the corner of my eye, I see the barrel of a gun next to my right eye. I knew that Brent was behind me, and I was also on target. The Taliban dude stood up and I squeezed the trigger. I heard just a millisecond later the report of Brent's gun going off and felt the heat of it. I jumped to my left, thinking that I'd been hit in the face.

Brent looked over to me where I'd sprawled away and said, "Stop being a bitch and get back up here!"

I stared at him and said, "Back up some."

"I didn't shoot you. It's just the hot gas."

"I don't care—"

"Shut up and shoot."

I moved away from him. I knew that he was right, but still, trying to fire with another weapon going off inches from your eyes doesn't make things easier. He was getting in some good shots, though, taking out a couple of guys.

Third squad had taken advantage of all this and they were on their way, sprinting toward that pile. I was concerned about cutting off my fire with those guys running toward the target. I used a quick guide to make sure I didn't take any of them out. If I put my hand out in front of my face, the knuckle of my thumb is on the target and the knuckle of my pinkie finger is the limitation of fire. I figure guys can cover that much ground. We'd taken out enough of the shooters that third squad was able to overrun their position.

A few moments later, we got the all clear over the comms. We walked up to assess the damage and count the kills. I saw that most of the guys got taken out by head shots. If they'd gone down due to chest shots, we wouldn't have seen much at all: a little hole in the front then a golf-ball-size exit wound. With the rounds we were shooting, though, the exits were bigger than our fists. Most of the head shots

were completely clean, with the face hanging over an emptied skull. We finished that count, took the necessary photos, and then stood there for a minute.

"Why'd they even do that?" I asked.

Brent stood next to me, toeing the ground, his breathing
now returned to normal. "We're Americans. We're the enemy."

"Stupid. What good did it do them?"

The question was left hanging. A few guys broke off from
our group and started walking toward the disabled truck.

Over the comms I heard them commenting and counting. They were surprised to find four dead in the truck—
the driver, a passenger in the front seat, the gunner, and his
loader assistant in the back.

Rice's voice came to me, admiring and proud, "We got
them. Goddamn if we didn't get them."

I hustled over there, wanting to congratulate Rice on his
actions. He'd really stepped up. He was surprisingly calm,
especially compared to how he'd been acting just minutes
earlier. He reached into a pocket and took out a tin of long-
cut Copenhagen. He looked for a minute like he was going
to sneeze, but he seemed to wrestle that thing down and
then spit. He nodded me over toward him.

"Dude. I'm not going to say this to anybody but you."
He looked around to see who else might be within earshot.

"What?"

"I didn't mean to shoot who I shot."

"Doesn't matter."

"No, dude, it does. C'mere."

I followed him around to the front of the truck.

"See?" he said.

I looked and then I realized what he was talking about. A round had pierced the left side of the front windshield. Drivers in Afghanistan sit on the right-hand side and drive on the left, just like they do in England. Rice was saying that he'd gone after the driver, but instead he was actually aiming at the passenger.

"Luck, man. Pure luck. Must have been one of those magic bullets bouncing around in there, and took the driver out."

"Who cares, man?" I said, gripping his biceps and shaking him slightly. "You took out a freakin' rolling machine gun nest for us. That's what counts."

Rice nodded. "Roger that."

We formed up again and advanced on our target. Intel came in that he was still at the same objective. Then Bruno and Sergeant Val did a quick search around the perimeter of the building, paying particular attention to the doorway we were going to breach. The Taliban had learned that we would stack up on doorways, so they'd begun placing explosive charges waist high that could be remotely detonated. The dog didn't hit on anything so we were good to go. If he had, then we had multiple options—another entrance or even get a C-130 crew to drop a bomb on the building.

While the assault team was checking things out, Brent, Rice, and I made our way to our hide. We had to climb a building to gain access to the roof, approximately forty feet above us. Rice was going to assist with the ladder.

"Whatever you do, don't move this thing." I had visions of Brent and I trying to exit through the building's interior, navigating multiple stairways—that was not something we wanted to take on.

Brent was an excellent climber. He enjoyed rock climbing and worked out on indoor walls whenever possible. I let him take the lead up the ladder. He ascended quickly, and try as I might, I lagged behind a little. Before I got to the top, I heard Brent's voice, a whisper. I figured he was telling me to pick up the pace. When I got to the top, I could see that he wasn't alone and I could hear that he wasn't talking to me. A figure stood twenty or so feet ahead of him, and in Pashto, Brent had told the figure to stop.

Without turning around, Brent said, "Cover me. Cover me."

I hadn't gotten on the roof yet; I was still looking over the ledge. I slung my rifle around and scoped the guy, right in the middle of his forehead. Brent had his pistol drawn and it appeared that the man he was confronting was unarmed. At that point, another man came out onto the roof and he was speaking. Given how quiet the night was, it sounded like he was shouting, whether at Brent or to his buddy I couldn't say. I wanted him to just shut the hell up. Who knew what he was saying; he could have been giving our position away to a sniper.

Brent talked to them, and using sign language, he pointed his pistol at their faces and then down at their feet, got them both to lie facedown on the flat roof. He indicated that they should stay right where they were or they were going to get shot. We radioed security and a guy came up and detained them there for the duration of the mission.

We were only on an intermediate roof at that point, roughly twenty feet in the air. A second part of the building rose approximately the same distance.

"Get the ladder. We're going all the way up," Brent said.

"I don't think that's a good idea. We've got a view from here. We need to keep an eye on these guys." The last thing I wanted was for them to go back inside and return with weapons or reinforcements. I also didn't want to tell Brent that I was not wild about heights. Rather than debate the issue, I leaned out over the edge and pulled the ladder up. We didn't have too much room to extend the ladder's base, so it was nearly vertical. All I could think of was leaning the wrong way and crashing down on my back or tumbling all the way over the edge to the street below.

Stateside, we used to call Brent "Ninja." On weekends, he'd be out drinking and come back dressed in this tight-fitting all-black polypropylene suit with a balaclava/hood on it. He'd wrap a rag around his face and run through the hallways doing back flips and other gymnastic stunts. One of his favorite pranks was to come into your room at night, dressed as a ninja, and simulate cutting your throat while you slept and then slip out of the room. In my mind, he kind of ninja-flew up that ladder with no problem at all. I followed him and we still had another ways to go. I started to retrieve the ladder and Brent stopped me.

"No. We'll free-climb from here."

My heart skipped a beat. "I can't do that."

"Sure you can." He pointed at a set of metal stairs that led up to the top of this section of roof.

I looked back toward the objective and the assault team was just placing the C-4. Over comms I heard that they had a thirty-second count until they blasted it.

"Take a picture."

"What?"

Brent had his digital camera out.

I could hear the count go down to twenty. Brent was waving his camera at me. "C'mon. Last deployment. I may never do any of this again. None of my buddies will believe I did this kind of crap."

I did as he asked, first checking to be sure the flash was off. He had already taped over it. I got him in various poses, thinking this is not how Pemberton and I would normally do things. We heard a sharp crack off in the distance, maybe four hundred meters away.

Over the comms, I heard the leader of the assault team say, "Screw it. We're breaching out. We're breaching out."

The crack had been followed by a tracer round arcing over our heads. I knew that someone had spotted us. Inside the objective, loud pops and flashes were going off. Below me, in the direction where the tracer came from, I saw a low wall, maybe four to four and a half feet tall. A man was running back and forth. With trees in between his position and ours, I had a slightly difficult time sighting on him. Every few seconds, a round would come up from that location, making its way through the trees and near enough to us that we both were amazed.

"How is he doing that?" Brent sounded more mystified than angry.

"I don't know, but we have to take a shot. Make sure he doesn't go after the guys in the objective."

Since we'd been fired at, the ROEs (Rules of Engagement) were clear. We could defend ourselves.

"I don't think I can hit that." Brent lowered his rifle.

"I don't either."

All that was visible from that height and angle, and with the wall, was the very top portion of the man's head and a bit of his shoulders. He was basically sprinting and the trees would offer some protection. Eventually he slowed his pace, but he kept the muzzle of his AK on the top of the wall angled up toward us, holding steady while he fired a fairly steady stream of rounds our way.

I knew he was getting more confident the longer he was down there and we weren't returning fire in his direction. His shots were getting closer, more dialed in on us. Brent was old school. He had his laser range finder, his Mildot Master cards, and he was working his papers to get a calculation done. Then he got out a mini range finder and sent that laser out onto the wall.

"I got 413. 4–1–3."

I dialed in to that distance. "Got it."

"Sounds about right to me," he said, checking his papers.

"I'm going to lead him 1.5 mil."

I squeezed as gently as I ever had, wanting to keep that Mildot right in the center of the top of his head. As I was squeezing, he was firing off a few more rounds at us. My bullet must have struck home because the AK flipped in the air and then clattered to the ground. The rounds stopped coming in on us.

I shook my head in disbelief. "That was the luckiest shot of my life."

"Dude, you got him."

"Can't believe it."

We called the kill in and we were glad that we'd eliminated one bit of danger. It sounded like they had their hands full inside the building. At least they knew that when they exited the building no AK rounds would be coming at them.

When we heard the all clear, I sat down cross-legged on

a heating and cooling duct with my rifle across my lap. Brent was lying on his back with one leg pretzeled and resting on the opposite knee. We both stayed there sky gazing and looking out over the Kandahar skyline. I could see a few flashes from tracer rounds, sparks catching all around the city. I remember being a kid and going down South to be with family, watching the fireflies, running all around trying to catch them and hold them. That night scene in Kandahar was almost as peaceful. It was strange to be above it all, knowing that firefights were going on all around. An occasional crump of an explosion disturbed the quiet. All I could think of was how good we had it Stateside. You could sit outside and admire the city lights and know that you weren't blocking things out, that everything was good and quiet and that those lights going on and off were televisions flickering and not a tracer round.

We made it back to the Brits' compound without incident. I was asked about that shot again and again, and all I could repeat was that it was a lot of luck and a little bit of good timing. That was true of most sniping shots, and we used to say that you just had to know how to use your good luck. Brent was incredibly cool and collected. I thought he'd be on a bit of a high since this was his first time getting rounds on targets. If it weren't for him constantly checking his camera to make sure his photos were still good to go, you wouldn't have known what he'd just done.

The Brits welcomed us back with some great show and

they projected *The 40-Year-Old Virgin* on a screen inside the compound. We all laughed, and only when I thought about it later did it seem strange that the night ended like that, a bunch of guys eating and laughing. The only reminder of what we'd done was the odor. We'd tried to clean that foul-smelling muck out of the treads of our boots, but some of it had gotten inside our boots. The medics came around and made sure that we took our doxi and I wasn't happy about it but I took my dosage. Nobody laughed when they were asked if they had swallowed. I knew firsthand what could happen if you accidentally ingested that kind of raw sewage. In Mosul, one of the troopers was running full out with his mouth open and ran through a cesspool. He was out of commission for a month at first, and I watched his gradual decline, turning yellow and then walking with a cane. He eventually recovered, but with his kidneys taking such a hit, he had to leave the army for good on disability.

One thing the guys said in Iraq was that they grew tired of getting what they called the "eat-shit-and-die" look we got all the time from the locals. Nobody ever acted on the hatred I was sure they felt, but that stare stuck with you. At least in Afghanistan, we weren't moving around among the people too much. With the curfew in effect, most civilians stayed put. That was what surprised me about the two men on the roof. That could have turned out way bad for them or for us, I guess. But they kept their mouths shut and did what they were told.

I'd soon have to do the same thing. Delta Force came in and Brent I were going to be roommates. I wondered how long it was going to be before the ninja struck again. Ours wasn't going to be the only big brother/little brother relationship. We had a long-standing and cooperative thing going with the Delta guys. I was curious to see how that was going to play out operationally.

9. Ninja Wife and the Big Bomb

A week after the rubble-pile ambush, I learned why some people call it the runs. I woke in the middle of the night with a sharp pain running across my lower abdomen; what some of my aunts and uncles down South referred to as the call of nature was more like a bloodcurdling scream. I scrambled out of bed, ignored Brent who sat in the bluish light of his computer monitor, and sprinted for the facilities. There, my bloodcurdling scream could be heard all the way into the Hindu Kush. Later, after I'd been down and out for more than twenty-four hours, one of the medics described my body's violent rejection of a seafood dinner as "violent diarrhea and explosive vomiting." I was so weak and so cold that I lay in bed beneath my Arctic layer, rated for twenty-five to thirty degrees below zero, shivering and sweating at the same time.

My teammates were less than sympathetic to my plight. I remember their puzzled expressions when I sat down at the table with that meal—I still can't use the words to label what I ate without feeling queasy—and dug in. I was raised in Maryland, and seafood was something I really missed. So when the guys came to my room and saw me in such a sorry state, an IV dripping into my arm and me buried beneath every cover I could scrounge up, they fake-whispered to Brent things like, "Keep it down. You know he can't."

"Hey, man, that's not cool making him the *butt* of our jokes."

"Don't be giving him any shit, he's got enough, I mean he's been through enough."

"Just let him know that this too shall pass, as my mom always says."

We'd not been out on an operation for a few days, so just as I was getting to the point when nothing else could leave my body, we got called in for a mission. Sergeant Atkins took one look at me as I dragged myself out into the hallway, and said, "I know you're not up for it, but we need you."

With the arrival of the Delta Force guys, our operational tempo became very interesting. Things were so hot, Delta would pick up some of the hits for us, mostly during the day, while we hit targets at night. We'd been so busy that we couldn't handle everything, so we were grateful for the help. Most of the Delta Force guys had been Rangers at one time, so we had a big brother/little brother type of relationship with another special forces group. It used to be, before the global war on terrorism (GWOT), that Rangers pulled security for them while they hit a target.

With the changing nature of things, the war on terror, everyone was spread so thin that we took on a more direct-action role and often worked in cooperation with them. I'd been looking forward to doing that.

For this one, though, it was just going to be our usual crew. As bad as I was feeling, after hearing that we were going to be dropped only two thousand meters from the objective, I figured I could suck it up and do this thing. If I needed to puke, I'd puke and then keep going. The medics had been overseeing my care and in addition to the IVs—I had three of them—they were giving me pills and an electrolyte fluid to get me rehydrated properly.

Bending over to put my boots on, I nearly started to cry. My back hurt so bad, and putting my head below my waist to lace up my boots brought back some of the nausea and head-spinning that had had me flat on my back for more than twenty-four hours. I took a short walk outside. Normally, I hated the heat and kept my room at a very cool sixty degrees. With all the shivering and stuff I'd been doing, the late-afternoon 110 degrees felt great. I was starting to come around a bit more.

Back inside, I looked at the big board and its maps and satellite feeds. This operation looked pretty straightforward. A small one-story building surrounded by three smaller huts, the compound itself shaped like an L. In all the images, though, we could see a large group of people, approximately twenty women and children and four or five males. I hated that. The Taliban fighters used women and kids as human shields. Taking guys out under those circumstances required precise shooting, and down in the mix of all that, an assaulter couldn't fire with the kind of timing and precision needed to avoid collateral damage.

Fortunately, there were several good positions from which Brent and I could fire, and the shots would only be in the seventy-five to ninety-five-yard range. Relatively easy shots with the only complicating factor being who else was going to be moving around and among the bad guys. A storage shed was nearby the main house and that was where I planned to set up. After a few more minutes of look- ing at all the images, I walked back upstairs to pack. I was so weak that I knew I'd have to travel light. Downgrading my ammo was one way to do that, and I chose to only take two magazines. If I needed more, Brent would be able to supply me. I loaded up on water and hydration packets, figuring that if I was out of commission healthwise, then no amount of ammo would matter.

I sat through the mission brief slugging down canteens of water and hydration fluids, trying to stay focused. I knew I couldn't make any kind of sense, so I had Brent do our part of the brief. I could barely get through the whole brief, and just after Brent finished up, the commander walked in. We all stood at attention, and I could sense that I was having a hard time not weaving. He looked over at me and said, "Are you all right, soldier?"

"Yes, sir. Good to go, sir."

I knew my response didn't have any of that gung ho snap that it was supposed to have, but it did get me through. The commander spoke to us, talking about the fact that we only had three weeks left in our deployment and we'd be done and needed to finish up strong. He pointed out that our target was a particularly important one—another suicide vest maker. I was having trouble focusing on his words, drifting on some random thought. But when he got to the part about the strong likelihood that the compound was heavily loaded with HME supplies (home made explosives) and that we needed to be extra vigilant, I was right back there with everybody. There'd been a recent incident during which the Taliban set off a cache of explosives in a similar kind of compound, killing and wounding many civilians and then claiming that the deaths and injuries were due to an American airstrike or a mortar round. That was upsetting the locals as well as the folks back home.

Getting blown up was not the way I wanted to go out, and like most of the guys, the possibility of an IED or HME getting me was always in the back of my mind. I don't know if it was my weakened physical state, but as I sat there listening to the commander, all I could think of was that I wanted to get the hell out of that country and go home. We'd taken a lot more casualties than I'd ever experienced on my previous deployments. As we walked out of the briefing room and made our way to the vans, Brent was beside me, muttering, "This sucks."

The prop blasts and the diesel exhaust made it feel like the already hot air was on fire. I was barely able to make it into the belly of the Chinook, the force of those winds so battered me. I sat down and closed my eyes, unable to battle my sleepiness. I hadn't eaten anything since I'd gotten sick. The guys were amazed. My mom had just resupplied me with cans of ravioli and a five-pound bag of gummy bears. I used to amaze everybody by going through that whole bag in a couple of days. I'd tried with the gummy bears, but they'd clawed their way back up and out of me.

Brent sat down next to me. He wrapped his arms around me and hugged me, in a singsongy mom voice telling me, "There, there. It's okay, baby."

"Dude, not right now. I don't feel good and I don't need this crap from you."

I must have sounded really pissed because Brent backed off. "If you need to, man, we'll get you to stay on the helicopter. If things get bad, they'll set you down."

"No. I'm good. I can do this."

"All right. Don't slow me down though."

"Roger that."

Brent hit it on the head. I was torn because I didn't want to let the guys down by not being there to help them out, but I also didn't want to be a liability to any of them by not being able to perform at my best.

They all knew that I was struggling and throughout the two-thousand-meter run to the objective they offered words of encouragement and support. I should have figured that, even though we were getting dropped off so near to the objective, the pace was going to be really high—especially with the presence of all those explosives. We had to get there before anybody could detonate the stuff. I ran with my head down the entire time, puking a little bit, a thin liquid, carrying my rifle like it was a suitcase. A hundred meters from the compound the lead element of the assault force came to a complete and sudden stop. All their lasers lit up and the guys began a slow creep toward the target building.

Even in my sick fog, I knew that something was up. Normally, they would have kept up that high pace right to the objective. The whole surprise, speed, and violence of action thing was now out of sorts. They began signaling back to us that they had their eyes on somebody and he was very, very close. We kept advancing, and as I got past the corner of a building that was on the far outside part of the lower leg of the L, I could see the assaulters within ten feet of the man. He turned around, and then after we tried a few words of Pashto, he sprinted off shouting at the top of his lungs. That was followed by a tracer round going from the center of the compound straight up into the night sky, a clear signal to other bad guys that something was up.

Something definitely was up. Armed fighters streamed

out of that building and suddenly things were in total chaos. Women, children, and men were all running around scream- ing. It was impossible to sort and track who was who. Shots were being fired, and as we'd always said, once the first bul- lets fly, that plan you had goes to shit.

I made my way to the building I'd targeted and rested my ladder against it. I saw Brent flying at a dead sprint be- fore pulling up at his structure and mounting his ladder. We both took our positions. I saw him peering over the edge. He had his Glock out and I watched him as he scanned his roof, checking to be sure no one was up there, doing exactly what the manuals state you should be doing.

Brent, despite his being a joker, was generally a real by- the-book kind of guy. In one of our first balcony meetings, he told me about an operation that really reinforced for him the idea that rules are rules and shouldn't be broken unless absolutely no other option exists. His spotter had climbed onto a roof and didn't execute the scan and check the way he should have. As it turned out, he made contact with the enemy and was shot in the eye. Fortunately, he survived and was even able to take the shooter out. Brent was amazed, as was I, by that spotter's calm. He came down off the roof, walked over to some of the other team members and said, "Hey, guys, I got shot in the face. I need some help." He got the help he needed and recovered well enough to stick around in the army for another three years.

Unlike Brent, I didn't like using my pistol after a climb. I was interested in getting up there as fast as I could, and I wasn't as agile as the Ninja, who could climb with that pistol in his hand faster than me without one. I always thought that if I got to the point where I could see someone on the roof I was about to mount, I'd push the ladder back and fall to the ground. Better to get that kind of minor injury than to get shot.

On this trip to the top, I saw what appeared to be a pile of black clothes but nothing else. I got on the roof, dropped into a low-crawl position, and made a hard right to the far side of the building. From there, I spotted a man in the courtyard of the compound. He was peering around a corner of one of the buildings. The courtyard itself was muddy, looking like it had been freshly watered—soaked is more like it. He was looking toward our main objective, the main house where the assaulters had planned to be. I knew they were in proximity to that location because I could hear the nine-bangers and one-bangers going off, serving as a distraction to the enemy. Those devices sound like a weapon's discharge, but they have the added element of flashing lights.

I heard the sound of an AK going off, and looked down to see the guy I'd spotted firing randomly into the air, either to gain attention to his position or who knows what. I zoomed my scope all the way out, wanting to keep as close to him as possible while still being able to make out the environment around him. He was about eighty meters away.

At that distance, I'd normally have the zoom all the way in, tight enough that I could make out fine detail on him like a button on his shirt. In this case, that wouldn't be effective because I wanted to be able to track the position of the women and children in the courtyard. I also backed the elevation on the scope all the way out.

At this point, he was behind the building, just sticking the muzzle of the rifle out and firing randomly. I remember seeing that in the movie *Black Hawk Down,* and thinking it was a stupid tactic, that by firing all those rounds he could have possibly hit someone. I eased the safety off on my rifle, and fired at him, hitting him square in the chest. He dropped but then he raised his head and started screaming. Then I saw blood spurting into the air. I didn't wait to see him bleed out, but it was clear he no longer posed a threat.

I continued to scan, and out of the corner of my eye, I saw that black pile of clothing move. I figured it was the wind or maybe my fever delirium had me seeing things. Someone from our team had cleared the body I'd shot, and I knew that nobody had thrown anything up on that roof either. I looked back and that pile started quaking again. I'd been down on my belly in a good firing position, so I rose to one knee to get a better look at what was going on. I thought maybe a chicken was up there. I'd seen different fowl on top of these low roofs a bunch of times before and a few cats as well. I edged closer to the pile and then I really thought I was seeing something. I was five feet from the pile when a human figure emerged, did a kind of cartwheel, got to its feet, and then sprinted across the roof before diving over the edge.

I hustled over to the edge. I couldn't tell if he was armed or if he had a bomb vest on or what, but I didn't want to shoot him, just get him to stop. I was pretty good at placing rounds right past someone's ear to let them know that they'd better freeze. This time, though, because of the downward angle from which I was firing, the bullet impacted just in front of him as he ran, kicking up a spray of dust and some clods of mud. He stopped in his tracks. I called the guys in and watched as they grabbed him, zip tied him, and herded him off.

I tried to calm down. I was breathing pretty heavily and was also pissed at myself for not having cleared that roof. Right where the pile had been, where that body emerged, was an AK. I could have easily bought it for not following procedures, but I once again got lucky. I have no idea why he didn't take me out. That didn't factor into my not shooting him, but I still wondered what the hell was going on. I picked up the AK and inspected it. A round was chambered so he could have easily fired it on me.

I called it up over the comms, letting the guys know that I was going to toss down that AK so they could collect it. That got the chatter going about a guy being up there, armed, and me not shooting him. A few guys commented on how lucky I was and how it could have gone really bad, really fast for me. I agreed and thanked my lucky stars and everything else that contributed to my heart still pumping blood.

I resumed my prone position as the guys did their investigation, making sure no one else was coming to join the fight. All the dead were collected in one spot, being photographed. Their weapons were checked, and photos of the magazines to show that rounds had been fired were taken, all to prove that we had been engaged by the enemy. A small team broke off and entered the building I was on top of. Sergeant Val brought Bruno in a few seconds later, and that dog started going nuts, barking and snarling. Everybody came running out of the building, coughing and screaming up at me, "Irv! Jump! Irv! Get off that thing!"

I was so out of it that I knew even that short jump could mess me up, so I got down the ladder as fast as I could, grabbed it, and got fifty feet away as fast as my rubbery legs could carry me.

Simmons, one of the assaulters, came up to me, shaking his head. He put his hand on my shoulder and leaned in close, his face distorting in my vision.

"You were sitting right on top of a cache of IEDs, explosives, and a bunch of chemicals and fertilizer."

Dorsey, who frequently worked with the C-4 we used, added, "Highly, and I mean *highly*, unstable compounds. Fire a shot into there and the whole thing goes—" He lifted his eyebrows and put his hands together in front of him and then lifted them toward the sky like a mushroom cloud.

I shook my head, not wanting to believe what they were saying. "No way."

"See for yourself—" Dorsey stood sideways and swept his arm in the direction of the hut.

I peered inside and it was mind-blowing to see all that stuff in there. Grenades, RPGs, stacks of fertilizer bags, jars and boxes of chemicals, buckets of nails and screws and other scrap metal all stacked and piled from floor to ceiling.

I stepped away and stood off staring into the sky. Twice in one day. First the cartwheel man, as I called him, hadn't shot me in the back when he'd had the chance, and there I was on top of thousands of pounds of explosives and none of these guys had detonated them. I didn't want to think about it anymore, but everybody else did. I couldn't blame them.

I heard a bunch of voices, but couldn't keep track of who was speaking.

"Wait a minute, the dude on the roof—"

"The one who jumped off—"

"The route he was taking could have put him right in that doorway."

"Why'd he stop?"

"That warning shot. What would have happened if—"

I came to the conclusion that the guy wanted to take out more than just me. He could have shot me, but if he'd gotten off the roof and back into the building, he could have done a whole lot more damage.

Fortunately, we had more work to do. We'd killed three of the MAMs (military-aged males) and captured another pair. One of them was our objective and he was fairly high ranking. I figured he had to be. We'd uncovered weapons and explosives caches before, most every time, in fact. But nothing compared to this. There was enough stuff there that they could have planted IEDs along every roadway and every doorway in Kandahar. We also found a burlap sack of heroin, little plastic bags of what looked like black tar.

The whole experience just put me in a bad place mentally. I watched as the assaulters rounded up the women and children. Some of the women they had to zip-tie and fingerprint, and who knew if they were sympathizers of the Taliban, whether they were there out of fear or having no other options. I don't use the word "hate" very often or experience that feeling, but looking at those kids, I thought of my sister's kids, my nieces and nephews, and I almost broke down, thinking about what those Afghan kids and those women's lives were like. How the hell could those "fighters," and I had to question my use of that word to describe these guys, use women and children like that?

I wasn't a father, but I'd seen how some of the guys with

kids reacted. Once, in Iraq, a man had held up a child as a shield, clutched it to his chest as a way to keep from getting fired on. One of the assaulters I was working with had come into the room, saw the man, saw the baby, saw the man's AK tucked in the crook of his arm and still pointing at us, and he put two in the guy's face. I could see the anger and the hatred in my fellow soldier's eyes, and I couldn't judge him or his actions.

That night, I saw Brent, the big prankster hard-ass, walking among the women and children. The kids crying and the women wailing and rocking just tore at your soul. Mentally, I understood their response. We had just come into where they lived and had shot some of the men they knew and loved. I wished that they could have understood why we were doing the things we were doing. We all wanted them to not be afraid of us, but how could they be anything but afraid? One kid was inconsolable. His mother was shielding him, and I could tell she was even more afraid of what we might do if she couldn't get this kid to stop crying. He was maybe two or three years old tops, and Brent walked up to him. He knelt down and reached into his pocket and took out a chem light. He showed it to the kid who turned away and kept screaming. Brent cracked the light stick and it started to glow. He waved it around in the air and the kid saw the light and turned toward it.

A few seconds later, with a stick in his hands, that kid wasn't crying anymore. I didn't know that kid's whole story; maybe he'd lost a father that night and a chem light was a poor substitute for what he might have lost. It definitely couldn't make up for the impoverished conditions in which he lived. But for at least a few moments he was calm. I'd seen guys do things like that all the time. We all did it at one time or another, and knowing how horrible it all was and how confusing and frustrating just made the job so much tougher.

Once, in Iraq, one of my buddies had had to shoot an older woman. It wasn't a case of mistaken identity. He knew what he was doing, but he had no choice. He saw her inside a building, moving around with several AK-47s going into and out of several rooms. We were taking heavy fire, and she got killed. What's worse, we took several captives and one of the guys confessed to being her son. He told the interrogators that he was the one who was supposed to be helping supply the shooters, but he asked her to do it, figuring that we wouldn't shoot her. He'd been hiding inside the house, under a bed, while his mom did his job for him.

There was one young male, we couldn't determine exactly how old he was, but we decided to let him go rather than detain him. He looked like he was maybe fourteen or so, beardless and with these eyes that gave him a dazed expression like he was in a total state of disbelief. We told the other women to get him out of there, and that they should all go to the next village or wherever but to stay the hell away from this place. I was hoping that giving that kid a chance and treating him with some respect might make him think twice about us and about Al Qaeda and about the whole messy situation.

At that point, we knew that we had to destroy that weapons cache. When we discovered a small one, it was no big deal for us to dispose of it. Given how large that supply was, we called it in and the command ordered in an F-16 to drop a five-hundred-pounder on top of that cache. We had to get out of there, but we all wanted to see that bomb go off. The Chinooks had been able to make it within three hundred meters of our location, so I didn't have as far to walk. I sat down and instantly smelled my own clammy funk. Whatever toxins were in my system, they seemed to be leaching out of me. I sat down and lifted off my night vision and took off my helmet and just cradled my head in my hands and tried to breathe deep.

I don't know how much time elapsed, but I was jostled awake. I could hear over my earpiece that the F-16s were coming in. I shuffled to the end of the craft, trying to get a glimpse of the impact over the gray outlines of my guys. All of us craned our necks for the light show that was just about to take place. The F-16 came in afterburners going and dropped down. We could see the bomb and by the time it made contact with the ground, the F-16 was already winging away. We started a countdown in synch with the pilots.

"Five."

"Four."

"Three."

"Two."

Before we got to one, the bunker buster connected and dirt rose up in the sky like a geyser and then we faintly heard and then felt the concussion as the bomb and that cache exploded. Over the comms I heard the F-16 crew laugh and ask, "What the hell did you guys find down there?"

I was wrong about my estimate of how many explosives and bomb-making materials there were in that cache. I was later told that it was likely we'd hit on a major supply depot for all of southern Helmand Province. It had been operational for a number of years. All I could do was hope that it was out of commission for good, that we'd put a serious dent in the Taliban's capabilities.

I had no idea what the value of the heroin we destroyed was. I knew that the money would have been used for more supplies to make more IEDs and HMEs. And I knew that there weren't enough bunker busters in the world to take out all those fields of poppies.

To say that I was starting to feel disillusioned is pretty accurate. I still believed that we were doing the right thing by being there and taking on these forces, but the toll was climbing. I'd lost some good friends, and I knew that it wasn't just the fact that my resistance was low due to the

food poisoning that had me thinking that there was something rotting away in that country. I'd felt the same way in
Iraq, had begun to question why we were putting in so
much blood, sweat, and tears in a place where people didn't
seem to want our help or care that we were losing lives in
the process. I think that for most of us, you could only go
out there and put your head down and just do your job and
not question anything for only so long. It seemed like more
than in Iraq, the strangeness of my experiences in Afghanistan threw questions into my face so that I couldn't ig-
nore them anymore.

A few days after we destroyed that weapons cache, we
were out on another operation. Brent and I were on the
outside of a compound, placing our ladders to climb over a
fifteen-foot-high wall. Our ladders were extended, and we
each had our pistols out—I'd followed through on my
promise to do that—and we were just about to start our
climb when a black-clad somebody or something came flying over the wall. I could hear the wind snapping the fabric
of the black burqa that flapped around what I had to assume was her. She landed with her feet spread and her
body turned sideways, looking like she was a skateboarder
steadying herself and then she did a combat roll and got to
her feet. She turned toward us and I could see the veil and
the mesh she wore to cover her face and eyes that sure
looked to me like a woman's. She sprinted off into the field
and disappeared down an embankment.

I looked at Brent and he looked at me.

"What the fuck is going on?" he whispered.

I climbed up the ladder and looked over the other side, hoping to see another ladder, some stacked lumber, something that woman could have used to get over that wall.

Nothing.

After the mission was over, we checked with the ISR guys, and they confirmed that what we'd seen was caught on a drone's camera. Someone had come up and over that wall and then disappeared into the terrain.

I kidded Brent. "It had to be your future ninja wife."

"Figures. She got one look at me and she ran off."

"Thermal couldn't pick her up either."

"Cold. Cold bitch of a woman. I'm better off."

10. Winding Up and Winding Down

Just as happened when I was working with Pemberton, Brent and I went out on other operations besides the more eventful ones I've described. By the time the end of July rolled around, I'd reached a total of more than twenty-five kills. Given that I was on short time at that point, the number that was most on my mind was how many days I had left before I would return to the States. I don't think I can begin to describe the grinding nature of the work, how it seemed like the sun and the sand infiltrated all your gear, took the shine off what was new, and made every movable part of your body and soul more resistant to its natural fluidity.

To offset that, as the days for our departure fell into the single digits, guys' spirits seemed to lift. Sure, that short-timer's mentality that I mentioned earlier was a part of it as well—the dread feeling that you were this close to getting out of the country and how much of a shame it would be if something happened that close to the finish line. If we said that this sucks, this really sucks, and this really, really sucks, then to get killed or wounded when you could measure time within the expiration date on a carton of milk would suck exponentially.

We also found ourselves in a bit of an anticlimactic situation as well. We'd all come into the deployment together, but for various reasons we wouldn't be leaving at the same time. A few guys left to attend to family matters. Davis and Johnson, two key members of the assaulters, both were scheduled to be married and got permission to go home early. Brent had been in country for two weeks before us, so he was going to leave before us by that same time span. He was excited about leaving, but the curse kind of hung over his head, and he kept telling me that he wasn't going to take the kinds of chances that he'd taken early on when we were first teamed.

I didn't spend nearly as much time with him as I had Pemberton, and we were so different temperamentally that we didn't get that close as friends, but I had a lot of respect for him. I admired how dedicated he was, and even if his downtime goofiness and his obsession with the video game the World of Warcraft sometimes mystified me, he was an outstanding teammate and someone from whom I learned a great deal.

I can't say that I had compiled a list of things I wanted to do before leaving Afghanistan, but one operation did stand out as a break from the usual routine. I'd heard about and seen photographs of the northern part of Afghanistan, its eastern border with Pakistan. Being from the East Coast and doing nearly all my training in Georgia, I hadn't seen real high-altitude areas and massive mountain ranges. I wouldn't get that chance, but on Brent's last mission with us, we did travel to a part of southern Afghanistan.

I also got to work with Rice one last time. He was still really into his role, and I admired him for that. He never complained about doing any of the grunt work he did in support of us. He'd already more than proved that he was a courageous guy, and it was no wonder really. I first met him when I deployed to Iraq for my initial overseas deployment. He was a door kicker back then and remained one for another year. We served in the same assault team back in Battalion. Breaching a door and being one of the first in on an assault team was pretty damn stressful. We all faced the unknown from time to time, but these guys' work role defined surprise, speed, and violence of action in a very real way.

He was along with us when we flew deep into the southern portion of Helmand Province the last week of July 2009. Because of the difficult terrain, we had landed five kilometers from the objective. Good thing Rice was along. He carried one of our ladders and an extra box of ammo each for Brent and me. Instead of desert or arid fields, we walked through an area of rocky outcroppings, first making our way along a trail that was defined by a sheer rock wall on one side and a hundred-foot drop on the other. A creek ran at the bottom of that ravine, and it was hard to imagine how it had carved and polished that wall, and how many eons it must have taken for it to do so.

With such a long walk ahead of us, I had the time to contemplate such things. I also did it to take my mind off the cold. It might sound funny to say that a temperature in the low seventies is cold, but considering that even during our nighttime operations we were moving around loaded with gear when it was ninety-five, the difference was substantial. I could feel the cool air rising up from the ravine and figured the water had to be very cold runoff from some mountains very far from where we were.

I was also thinking that we were very exposed. If we got ambushed, we were in a terrible fighting position. Our backs would literally be up against a wall, and the sides of that ravine were nearly perpendicular to the trail. There was no way we'd be able to gain any kind of handhold or foothold to keep from plunging into that rocky creek below. The trail had a few blind curves and switchbacks, and a few times, my heart rate picked up when I thought about what was just around that bend. Doing all this at night also complicated matters. I thought of Pemberton and his fall, and I wanted no part of that scenario again.

I was curious to see our objective in person. In the photos we'd viewed, it was by far the most substantial residence I'd seen there. It wasn't that large, only one story, and it sat on a rectangular foundation of one thousand to fifteen hundred square feet. What impressed me about its construction was its roof. It had semicircular clay tiles like I'd seen some homes in California had. It had a finished look and attention to detail that you'd expect of houses in the West, but didn't ever really see in Afghanistan where most of the houses had a do-it-yourself kind of vibe. I thought that it was the kind of place that I could see myself having as a getaway someday. We'd been operating in Kandahar for a while, and the smell and the cramped streets and the dirt and disarray were getting to me. Out there, the air reminded me of Georgia when we were out in the woods during our sniper school.

The house was surrounded by cultivated fields—not the opium poppy fields we were used to seeing, but some kind of grain. Instead of weedy stalks and round bulbs, it looked like long grass. As we neared the objective, the rock outcropping dropped away, and a natural platform presented itself and curved down toward that small village and its single house. We hadn't had to be as vigilant about keeping quiet as we normally did. The sound of rushing water below us and the infrequent sounds of rock falls masked our footfalls. With about three hundred yards to go, that changed. The various teams split off. Though that wall was no longer as tall as it had been, there was still a ledge we had to get up on. With only three feet of trail to work with, the ladders were at a steep angle. They were only twelve feet tall, but any slip meant that you would plunge backward, hit the trail, and bounce down into the ravine.

We made it up onto a fairly flat rock ledge with a great view of the compound below us. The breachers were doing their thing. I could see them packing the C-4 on an outer section of the stone wall that encircled the house. Once they had an opening, they'd storm in, clear the courtyard, and then get to the house itself. In a way this was almost like storming a castle with a moat and all that. Brent and I were scanning the courtyard and came up with a count of forty subjects, all of them appearing to be asleep in that courtyard. Since they were all lying down and all covered in blankets and things, it was impossible to determine the makeup of the group's gender and age.

We were maybe fifty meters from that wall, a typical distance for a direct action sniper, so I was feeling really comfortable with that wide-open view and easy shooting distance. Over the comms we got the word to take cover. That concrete and stone wall was approximately two feet thick, so it was going to take quite a blast to knock down a section of it. They were going to use a fairly large block of C-4 with water packets behind it to make a shape charge that could cut through nearly anything. We listened for the countdown and then heard the explosion. I waited for a few seconds before looking, and the dust was just beginning to clear. I switched to thermal imaging so I could detect the heat signatures of the people in the courtyard, and they were all still lying still.

I'd seen this all before, but it still amazed me that people could sleep through that commotion. I counted three of our guys getting in past the wall and into the compound before any of the enemy began to stir. Then a few at a time got up and started to move to different parts of that enclosed area and then people started running around all over and it was like trying to keep track of which flake was which in a snow globe. Brent and I scanned all the targets, calling them out.

"I've got John Wayne," he said of the guy in boots.

"Checkered scarf," I added.

We went through each of them, giving them names based on identifying characteristics. I was scanning from their hands to their faces, first to see who might have a weapon and then to check their facial expressions. Anyone who looked calm, given the circumstances, was someone to focus on and track, especially if their eyes were moving around a lot, surveying the space. We were transmitting all this over the comms, helping the assaulters bring everyone under control. After a few minutes, the compound had settled.

I noticed movement at the far end of the enclosed area. He came from the direction of the house, tore around a corner, and was running fast and shouting. I couldn't see any weapons on him, but I wanted to send him a message. I cranked off a round in an open area in front of him, warning him to stop. He didn't, so I fired off five more in quick succession. Finally he stopped, and as soon as he did, two of our guys brought him to the ground, and then once he'd calmed down, they led him off away from the rest. The guys compared him to the photo of the target we'd come after, and he wasn't a match.

A small team had broken off from the assault element and were searching the house. Brent and I continued our exchange of information about the detainees in the courtyard, still not convinced that none of them posed a threat. Finally, they got the guy they were looking for. This had been a capture mission. The target was related to a high-value target. We were to bring him in and let the intel guys work with him. We packed up and were forming up for the long walk back. We could see from the ISR (Intelligence, Surveillance, Reconnaisance) footage that we'd woken up quite a few people. We could see them making their way toward our location. It was impossible to see if they had weapons, but based on how much contact we'd been having throughout this deployment, we all wanted to get the hell out of there immediately.

Though it was against protocol, Brent and I stood up against the rocky backdrop. We needed to be able to see a thousand meters out to make sure all was clear. We were exposing ourselves but there was no other way to secure that kill radius. We grabbed Sergeant Val and Bruno and exited in the same order as we'd come in. Ahead of us, a group of about twenty other Rangers were in the lead. I was on point for our small team, Brent behind me, the handler and dog behind him, with Rice on our tail. We took the same trail. We'd started the mission at 0300 and it was now coming up on 0700. The sun was balanced on the horizon and the pale gold light made it easier to see all the features of the land.

Over the comms, we got word that ahead of us a few hundred meters, around the first right turn in the rock face, three men were approaching. They appeared to be unarmed. Platoon Sergeant Atkins made the call that we would push straight through them. Subdue them if we had to but keep moving out. The last three thousand meters of our exit would take us through an open field with a line of trees and other tall scrub vegetation to our right. We were concerned primarily about that stretch and our vulnerability to ambush.

We were two hundred meters shy of that first turn when we heard the guys in the lead starting to shout. By the sound of it, our guys weren't yelling at those men to get down, they were screaming in surprise and anger. Suddenly, a laser beam came flashing down the very middle of our formation. I heard a loud snap as well, and I knew we were in it. Our three lead guys started firing and their three returned it. Because of how we were positioned on that ledge, with a right-hand turn in front of us where the three bad guys had a firing position, we really needed left-hander shooters to get the most effective angle. We were firing, but we knew that we weren't getting anywhere near on target. Their rounds were snapping over our heads and we were screwed. We couldn't move right or left to improve our angle, and going forward would have been suicidal. We would have had to somehow advance over our own guys and in doing so risk opening ourselves up.

I looked back. Bruno and Sergeant Val were down in the prone position. The dog was emitting a low, guttural growl. He was trained as an attack dog as well as a detection dog, and he knew the bad guys were over there. So did Brent. He looked like a sprinter preparing to get into the starting blocks. His gaze was directed beyond me, focusing on some point in the middle distance.

Atkins was on the radio and he was clearly pissed off.

"What the hell kind of intel was that?"

We were all collected on this narrow ledge, like ducks in a row. One lucky shot could have taken out several of us. If the Taliban shooters put one round close to that wall, because of the aerodynamics in that little corridor we were in, it could hug that wall and follow its contours. We couldn't press up against the wall for protection, so we had to hang out there. A few of our guys were hit. Their screams through the comms made me sick to my stomach. I could hear our M4s being discharged but still couldn't see our guys out in front.

"Snipers! Get up there and kill those motherf---ers right now!" I'd never heard Atkins lose his calm tone before in the three years I'd worked with him. Brent was on it, moving in a dead sprint to the front of our formation, yelling, "Let's go! Let's go!"

I joined him, and both of us had to scramble over the backs of our guys who were all in a prone position on the path. Just as we got to the front, the handler released the dog. I watched as he tore up that path, stepping on guys, weaving in and out, until he was right alongside us, just at the point where the wall made a jog to the right. I heard the handler yell out a command and that dog just came to a halt, its back legs coming up off the ground. It sat there barking. The three Taliban shooters had stopped firing, so I peered around the corner. They were just finishing reloading, and as soon they were, they began firing again.

Our guys who'd been engaged in a nearly face-to-face three-on-three firefight with them had somehow gotten out of it unscathed. A black *kameez* lay on the path, and all three of them were firing into it, round after round. The adrenaline rush of it all had them so hyped they were nearly out of control. The black fabric was flapping around and I figured they'd put so many rounds into him, there wasn't much of a body left. I thought it was strange that the dog, after the handler gave him the attack command, sprinted right past that pile on the ground. Brent and I led the assault team forward and twenty-five meters in front of us was a dirt mound. We climbed it and got a good view of the terrain. A narrow opening in the rock, about the size of a garage door, led into an open field. The dog had gone through that opening, crashed through some brush, and was pursuing two men. Brent and I got scopes on them and one of the men was naked.

The black *kameez* was his. Why he had discarded it we had no idea, except that maybe he could run faster without his legs being restricted by it. We didn't have time to ask why our guys had opened up on it thinking a body was in there.

Atkins had called in for an AC-130, asking for 105 mm howitzer shells to be dropped on all the targets we'd been engaging. The pilots confirmed three targets. They'd gotten out of our easy firing range and Brent and I just shook our heads, letting the other guys know that we wouldn't be able to get a good calculation on them at that distance and at the speed they were going. The pilots confirmed again their three targets.

"Three?" I asked Brent.

"I've only got two. You?"

"Two."

Then it hit us, the dog was still in pursuit.

Before we could say anything, I heard Atkins say, "Acknowledge. You're clear to engage."

My heart was in my throat. Sergeant Val had joined us at the edge of that opening, that gap in the rocks, and his expression said it all. He'd heard the order and he knew that his dog was done for. He kept licking his lips and his eyes were darting all around, and I knew he wanted to do something, we all did, but there was nothing we could do at that point. We could hear the bombs whistling down and the handler yelled, "You're going to kill him! What the fuck!"

I was feeling this complicated mixture of emotions and responses. I was in awe of the fact that we could call in an attack like that. An AC-130 gunship, flying thousands of feet in the air at hundreds of miles an hour, could pinpoint those small targets and drop bombs on them. On the other end of the spectrum, we had a dog whose trainer had enhanced his natural courage and loyalty. They were meeting in that place, and I hated the idea of that dog losing his life, we all did.

I couldn't believe what I saw in the next minute. The dog, Bruno, was still running all out after these shooters. Instead of taking a straight line, though, it was as if he could hear the direction the bombs were coming in from and calculated where they'd impact. He was weaving while these small explosions were kicking up dirt all around him.

When Bruno heard Sergeant Val call his name and give him the recall command, he put on the brakes, turned around, and made his way back toward us. When he was within fifty meters or so, he got another hand signal as a command and low-crawled the rest of the way before he jumped into his handler's arms. I'd never seen anything so cool in my time as a Ranger.

I could hear Atkins on the comms telling us to push up. The shooters had taken a position inside the trees and resumed firing at us. I had a few moments of doubt about my willingness and ability to go charging into the spray of gunfire. I kept flashing back to that incident with the Chechen and seeing all the casualties we'd taken and buddies getting killed. Human nature and instinct has to be overcome. Your first reaction isn't to go running into a wall of lead like that.

Brent didn't give it a thought. Even though he was on his last operation on his last deployment of his entire army career, he stood up immediately and ran forward. I watched him for a few seconds, figuring he was going to go down in an instant, but he kept going. I joined him. Behind me, the rest of the unit was filtering out from behind that rock and into the gap, making a hard right turn and forming up in a straight line, presenting ourselves to the enemy as a larger force than we were.

Something didn't feel right to me. We were advancing pretty easily. I started thinking about some of the old war movies I'd seen while also reviewing what was taking place. Three guys had taken us on, a unit of forty well-armed men. One of the guys was unaccounted for, but two of them were ahead of us in a fairly well protected area of heavy vegetation and trees. Normally, the Taliban we'd encountered wouldn't flee. They'd stay there and put up a fight. Something wasn't adding up.

"Eyes open. Eyes open," Sergeant Atkins ordered.

He was thinking what I was. Brent and I dropped down but continued to advance through the heavy underbrush, angling off from the main element. The tree line was clearly visible and through the tangle of branches we could make out some shapes inconsistent with the terrain. The guys in the AC-130 and the guys back in the TOC watching the drone footage confirmed what we suspected. We were being led into a trap. They were informing us that a large element was gathered behind that tree line in a small clearing. With their thermal detection apparatus, they were able to confirm that approximately twenty to twenty-five fighters were gathered. Based on what I'd seen in the past, I knew what they were observing—a round ball of white with a long dark stick. The steel of their weapons would show up as that dark bit, while their bodies radiated heat. Based on the outlines of those dark shapes, they knew that the element we were encountering was armed with RPGs, AK-47s, and what appeared to be an RPK, a small machine gun.

They were all trying to conceal themselves by wearing dark clothing, just as our multicam uniforms were giving us some protection.

"Sergeant Atkins. We have eyes on them. Permission to engage?" I asked.

"Acknowledged. Clear to engage."

Brent and I both began laying down fire into the tree line, raised up on one knee to get a better sight line and angle of fire. We knew that cutting through that underbrush and tree limbs was going to cause a lot of deflection, but we hoped to get lucky and take some guys out. Watching through my scope, I heard Brent's rifle fire and I followed that up an instant later. Turned out we were going after the same target and the man fell before my round could arrive. Brent got that one, and then I got a couple of others while he wounded another, a guy who was gut shot and barely able to crawl away. Hitting a man on the move through thick brush while shooting from the knee in full kit wasn't an easy task. We only had twenty rounds each and we'd already spent approximately fifteen for those three kills. We needed to turn that around somehow.

I contacted the machine gun team. The squad leader, Jameson, was a guy I started out with back when I was a cherry new guy, an eighteen-year-old with a desire to move beyond that role.

I said, "Bring your guys up."

I knew his guys were mostly about the age I was when I started. They made their way to our position and I looked each of them in the eye, and I could tell that there was a bit of fear there, but a whole lot more excitement and determination.

"Night vision on, guys. I'm going to put my laser on them. Wherever it goes, you fire."

I got a few "roger that" and thumbs-up.

The firefight was going on pretty heavy, but it seemed like, based on how far off target they were on us, they didn't really know the exact coordinates of our location. That was fine with me. I put my laser on where I'd last seen signs of the enemy shooters and from where I'd seen faint muzzle flashes. With three gunners putting out two hundred rounds in six- to nine-round bursts, they didn't have to be precision shooters.

I could see the excitement in their faces. They reloaded and went at it again. It was a rare treat for them to do this kind of shooting in combat. Even with this being their first experience with hardcore shooting, their endless hours of training showed. They kept their eyes on targets, fired controlled bursts, and were taking guys out. They kept at it for several minutes, changing belts a second time. The noise was so loud that I didn't really make out everything coming over the comms. After they'd emptied that third set, it got a little quieter. I heard what sounded like a lawn mower engine coming in from my right. I looked up and saw an A-10 coming in, its nose in a shroud of smoke. The tree line and the vegetation seemed to catch on fire, lit up in a hot white light as if thousands of Fourth of July sparklers were going. Those huge 20 millimeter rounds just shredded that area. The A-10 came in again, and I watched it dive, nearly vertical, toward that clearing, and it seemed as if the plane slowed in its descent from all that combined fire-power coming out of its guns.

The AC-130s also started firing off large explosive rounds and the ground beneath us went to jelly as the shells impacted and went off. I heard that the Chinooks were thirty seconds inbound and so we got ready to get the hell out of there, backing off and getting into our defensive posture prior to pickup. It was weird to think that this beautiful place, one of the few I'd seen that could be described that way, was being ripped up like that. Only a few hours before I was thinking that this was someplace that tourists would love to come and see. Brent and I decided to wait until everybody else was loaded before we ran. I could see Atkins in the rear on the ramp. He'd been doing a head count. He knew how many had come in and how many should be going out. If there was any kind of discrepancy in those numbers, the Chinook would be waved off. We weren't ever going to leave anybody behind. Atkins looked our way and pumped his fist up and down, signaling us to hurry up.

By making sure that everybody else was safely aboard, Brent and I had broken a rule—we should have mounted up immediately—but I did that sometimes either because I thought it was cool, I'd seen it in a movie, I was bored, or just got caught up in the moment. It was a stupid thing to do, but what the hell. By-the-book Brent felt the same way. We each squeezed off a few more rounds just for the hell of it.

Brent and I got into the Chinook, and the pilot got us out of there making all kinds of evasive moves to avoid gunfire and an RPG. I was scared and thrilled at the same time, watching the tail gunner jump back from his gun a moment after a long white trail of smoke flew past his position. He got back on his gun, and angling it hard and downward, opened up on the source of that smoke. I knew it was an RPG, and for some reason, I kind of half stood, half squatted, with my hands on the fuselage and my feet pressed into the floor, clenching my butt cheeks and squinting my eyes shut as hard as I could, foolishly thinking that if I braced myself that hard, the impact won't be so bad. Only no impact came. I opened my eyes and the gunner gave us a thumbs-up. That RPG had come within feet of the blades, and I knew there was no way that we would have survived a hit like that. Our luck was still running pretty good.

I'd only been with Brent for a few weeks, but he'd seen some pretty crazy stuff, and he'd more than stood up to the challenge. I guess we all wanted to go to war to test ourselves, and Brent's "don't hesitate, do my job right, and do it right away" attitude was more than admirable. The crazy thing was, as soon as we got back to the TOC, we downloaded our kit in the ready room and that was it for him. He had to hustle out and pack and get on the next plane out of there that same day.

We stood there, kind of awkwardly for a minute, neither of us saying much.

"That was my last one, man," Brent said. I couldn't really read his expression or his tone. The words came out almost like a question but not quite.

"Yeah. Unless you want to trade places."

"No. I need to get back. I've got a ton of paperwork to do and get everything situated. I'm going to be out for good in a month or so. I've got to get paperwork filed to get into school—"

I held up my hand to stop him. "I know all that. You told me a bunch of times. I was kidding."

"That's right. You're right."

He walked away, and I was left there wondering if he was having second thoughts; hell, it could have been ninth or tenth thoughts. I knew that he was going to miss it. I think that's why we both hung back there, why we didn't want to get aboard the Chinook.

I thought that was true until about a half hour later. The AC-130 pilot and the Chinook pilot were in the ready room hanging around. They wanted to show me the footage, so I sat with them for a while watching all the different images and feeds coming into the TOC. I was struck by the enemies' response to us bringing in that much firepower on top of them—from the air, from the machine guns. Guys just broke their discipline and were running around, looking for some route of escape. I kind of knew the feeling, on multiple levels and in multiple ways.

At the end, they showed us the footage of that RPG that whistled just past us.

"Too close for comfort," the Chinook pilot said.

The AC-130 guy just raised his eyebrows and cocked his head. "If you'd taken off half a minute or so before that—"

"Can't play what if in this game." The Chinook pilot's voice was hard and definitive. "Drive yourself nuts doing that." He paused and then laughed. "A buddy of mine back home used to say, 'If your aunt Agnes had balls, she'd be your uncle.' I never used to understand exactly what that meant."

I didn't say anything, but I was thinking about why Brent and I had delayed. I think we'd done it for the thrill, the rush, the smell of gunpowder in combat, the feeling of shooting in anger at an enemy bent on destroying us. It wasn't a conscious decision, really. I grew up in a family environment in which I heard over and over that everything happens for a reason. I didn't have an Aunt Agnes, and I did play the what if game a lot.

I got to say a brief good-bye to Brent before he dashed out to catch the van to the airfield and home. Just before turning in, I went to my locker. Taped to the top shelf was a picture that Brent had printed out. It was from the night we'd climbed those three different levels and he'd taken all those photos. Since he'd taken those images through his night vision, the picture was a bit hazy, like it was taken on a foggy night instead of the crystal-clear one I remembered. I appreciated the gesture, and I still have the photograph. I don't look at it at all. My memories of that night are sharper, better focused, and offer me more comfort. It may or may not be my imagination, but in my mind's eye, I remember seeing Brent standing on that roof, a line of stars above him, and a faint glint off his night vision lens completing the constellation.

11. Things That Go Hump in the Night

With Brent gone and the deployment winding down, the pace of our operations picked up a bit. With fewer snipers to cover the operations, I was kept on my toes. I picked up a few more kills, but we didn't engage in any major firefights. I was still hearing that I had as many as seventy kills, that I was this "little guy" who was on a crazy roll racking up kills. It would take some time after I returned for an accurate accounting, after all the AARs were reviewed and the other documentary evidence examined. I wasn't that into the number. Of course, I kept a mental tally, but I wasn't completely obsessed with it. It wasn't like the more enemies I took down the greater my chances of getting home safely increased. I was still working hard to do my job, but to be honest, that was getting increasingly difficult.

It was like the end of the school year. Some students were already done with their finals and had gone home. The instructors were all packing their things up, and so were we. I was back to living by myself, which was fine. I'd taken

to storing all my ammo and weapons and other gear in my
room. I wanted to cut down on the amount of prep time I
needed to go out. I'd had to do a couple of back-to-backs
and wanted as much downtime as I could possibly squeeze
in. I also knew that based on how things had happened
with Brent's departure, I could be out on an operation and
come back and have little or no time to pack to get out of
there for good.

I don't know why, but our final operations seemed to all
be taking place in and around Kandahar City, near what I
had described as that vacationland. I enjoyed that setting a
lot. I'd never been to a tropical island or anything like that,
and this was as close as I was going to get. The tall grasses,
the few trees that reminded me of palms, and the less intense heat without the sun's rays reflecting off the desert
sand, so different from the other parts of Helmand, all put
me in a good frame of mind.

The first week of August 2009 was my last in country,
and with most of my other teammates gone, I was eating
lunch with the rest of the squad leaders when all our pagers
went off. The sun wasn't close to setting at that point, and
I wondered how time sensitive this target was going to be.
I had a sense of what we were going to be tasked with. All
that day, a Thursday, we'd been tracking the movement of
a group of Taliban fighters. When we got the call and reported to the TOC, we watched the surveillance footage.
Since there was still daylight, the images were in color and

very sharp. We tracked their movements, noted the clothing they were wearing as identifying features of each member of the unit, and wondered again why it was that these guys were so lacking in discipline.

We knew that they understood that they were being observed from above. We had seen lots of footage of troop movements being halted and the men all gathering under blankets and clothing to avoid being detected from above.

Why this group didn't stay under the canopy of trees and vegetation more consistently surprised me. For a while they would, then they'd wander into the open for a bit, then duck back into the brush seemingly without rhyme or reason. Well, mostly without rhyme or reason.

I'd learned a few things about Afghan culture, and some of what was revealed took some getting used to, to be completely honest. There men interacted with one another in ways that would raise eyebrows here. They would walk along holding hands, would kiss one another as a greeting or as a good-bye. Sometimes those physical exchanges were more than just casual contact. At that point in the fighting, the U.S. military was working, advising, and training members of the Afghan National Army and Afghan Special Forces. Some of these guys had been around during the Taliban rule when the Pakistanis aided them, but most were recruited during the post-Taliban era and had first been trained by the British and now mostly by the U.S.

I had experienced working with the Afghan Special

Forces units over the course of a month and even lived near them. Then slept in tents just outside my building, but we had limited contact with them so they couldn't get any valuable intel from us. I also had some experience in Iraq in operating with Iraqi Special Forces, so I was accustomed to seeing locals in uniform. We also had to get used to another idea, what we came to think of as Man Love Thursday. We never talked about it much, but it seemed that pretty regularly on Thursdays, some of the Afghan army guys would engage in sexual activity with one another. We were used to the idea of "don't ask, don't tell" within our own military, so the only thing that made us really curious was, why Thursday?

I knew that in Islam Friday was the holy day of the week, and wondered if that had anything to do with it. Not that the Qur'an decreed it, but Thursday night was the equivalent of our Friday night, the last night of the work week, the night when you let loose in anticipation of the weekend. So, once we detected this pattern among those army guys, we basically steered clear of their residence area and gave them their privacy.

None of that would be noteworthy in regard to this mission, except that on several occasions our drone footage captured Afghan men in the field engaging in the same kind of activity.

As the squad leaders gathered to watch the videos, we talked about how most of us enjoyed fighting in the rural environments much more than in the urban ones. I was in total agreement with that. We trained heavily for urban combat, but I felt more like a real soldier out there in the fields and in the underbrush. Maybe it was all that reading about Vietnam that influenced me, but I also felt far less exposed out in the country than I did in the city. It seemed like in the city it was easy to find yourself cornered in some position. Out in the fields and even in what passed for forests, you always had multiple escape routes, or so it seemed.

We were told that one of the men in that group of twenty or so was a person of interest. To be honest, that was all I needed to know. I seldom paid close attention to the names and other brief histories we got about the guys we were going after. If the higher-ups said to bring him in, then that's what we were going to do. The rest was just clutter in my brain. I did want to know other details, like finding out if these guys were armed. As far as we were able to determine, they only had AKs. That was a good thing. I didn't want any more high-explosives drama in my life.

Once again, our battalion commander joined us before we went outside the wire, reminding us that this was one of the last missions we'd be going on and warning us against getting too complacent. That statement was unnecessary, but it struck me funny when we arrived at Kandahar Air Base. There were crowds of regular army, navy, marines, and air force guys all walking around the place. We sat there in the van looking out at them.

"I don't think it's Toby Keith again," someone said.

"He wouldn't come back so soon."

With the exception of all those guys being armed, we could have been at any concert venue anywhere in the U.S. Except sirens wouldn't go off and you'd have to take cover because some local was lobbing mortar rounds on you. It would have been nice to have been going to see some group playing, but at that point we were on a pretty tight leash. At one time or another, and with greater and lesser frequency, almost all the guys had snuck out of the compound. The one time I did, it was because a few of our guys had been KIA or WIA and command shut down our personal communications access, the MWR (morale, welfare, and recreation). I hadn't talked to my mom and dad or Jessica for a while, and given how bad everybody was feeling, our morale and welfare weren't going to get better by being further isolated. I burned through a bunch of calling cards but felt a hell of a lot better for having done that.

On the Chinook, nearing the objective, I looked out the window and spotted the most distinctive landmark of the area. Several spires, forty feet tall, made out of mud and shaped in a kind of staircase pattern, dotted the area. They reminded me of something aliens might have left behind. We landed two kilometers from our objective and we had to walk past one of those structures. I stopped and looked inside. Its outer shell had slits cut into it, which explained the appearance of a staircase, but it was essentially hollow.

Dirt and poppy leaves were piled inside; whether that was placed there intentionally or the wind had pushed it inside I wasn't sure. If they were silos, then they didn't offer a whole lot of protection to whatever you'd want to store inside them.

Just past that spire, the ground went from firm to squishy and a foul smell wafted up. The squad internal comms got crowded with guys asking what the hell was causing that smell. A few jokes about people's gas troubles had us cracking up, but then we all settled down when word came down that we'd just walked through a suspected Taliban burial ground. The smell of rotting flesh was disgusting but we were soon past the area and into the heavy vegetation. I took Killian, the weapons squad leader, with me, and we spread farther and farther to the right, with the main element keeping abreast of my pace.

We all adopted a kind of kick step to make our way through that terrain. If your toe came in contact with something that didn't feel like a rock or hard clump of dirt, something that had some give to it, you had to be prepared to fire. I hated the feeling that I could be walking past an armed fighter and getting blasted in the back. We'd been informed of this tactic, and had encountered it before, so that was why I'd offset myself and Killian a few hundred meters from the main group in order to overwatch. Using my thermals and night vision scope, I could detect bodies lying on the ground. To avoid any confusion between friendlies and bad guys, I had all of our guys keep their lasers on.

"Jimenez, five feet in front of you at three o'clock!"

A single shot rang out.

I repeated that same process three more times with different members of our element. We spent more than an hour going three hundred yards. At that point, I heard Bruno down in the brush with the assault force, starting to whine, getting really amped up and then barking nonstop. The guys were still focusing their lasers ahead of the formation, and just ahead of their light, I was able to make out a large dark shape, what could have been a boulder.

"I think I've got something."

A few seconds later, some of their lights were on it. They kept advancing toward it. I heard one of the newer guys, a kid named Dempsey, say that he'd detected some movement. A moment later he clarified his statement.

"Eyes on an RPK. Belt in place. Ammo boxes."

All hell broke loose. I could hear the repeated pops of weapons fire as the assault force began laying into the figures on the ground near the machine gun. I cracked off a few shots, but through the thick brush, the 175 grain projectile missed its mark. I was more helpful relaying what I could see from my position. Night vision relied on some ambient light to be present to give you the clearest view possible. Without it, as was the case in that thick vegetation, I could make out indistinct shapes and dark colors moving. Our guys were firing rounds, but I could see that about ten of the fighters had formed into a line. They were crouching, weapons in the hands of some, one hand on the shoulder of the guy in front, and they started moving off, looking like ducklings trailing after their mother. This wouldn't have seemed odd, except they were all naked. A small element had broken off and set up in order to kill or capture those that were fleeing. As soon as the group of naked, but armed, men exited the tree line, the small assault team met them with lasers right in the center of their chests. Once all of them were in the clear, the team put the men down at a relatively close range—twenty to thirty yards at best.

Our guys all had suppressors on their weapons so when they did discharge them, it sounded like a second grader clapping his hands together in three quick bursts, two in the chest and one in the head.

"One. Two. Three—" I heard over my earpiece as the guys counted the dead.

A moment later, I heard someone scream. I got eyes on one of the Taliban members twisting in the wind at the edge of the tallest clump of grasses and bushes, a dog hanging from his arm just above his elbow, its hind paws working to bring the guy to the ground. The man was in agony but he wasn't going to get loose from that dog's grip.

Briefly, the sound of an AK joined the chaos but it was quickly silenced. Intel from one of the air assets reported seeing lots of hot spots, which meant that guys were still bleeding out. Eventually, we confirmed that their entire element was dead.

I'd only fired two rounds, both of them designed to limit the enemy's movement, let them know that if they got out of that tangle of brush and bodies, I was there to end it for them. After I broke down my gear, I moved a bit closer to our element to better support them and provide better cover.

It was a gruesome scene. The guys had to disentangle the main pile, and document what had happened. To a man we agreed that what we'd seen was completely messed up. We wanted the hell out of there and had already called in for extract, but we had to do the job right.

"This did not just happen," Andersen said. He stood there pinching the bridge of his nose and shaking his head.

Some of our guys had taken out their white lights, their flashlights. Now instead of that indistinct out-of-focus scene that we'd been viewing, we saw the stark reality of it.

"I know you don't shoot a guy when he's pissing or shitting."

"Don't take a guy out in front of his family if you can help it."

"Let a man get up off a woman."

"This? What the hell is that?"

Galloway shone his light between the legs of one of the guys they'd had to pull apart from another. What looked like Saran wrap and a shoelace tied in a bow knot was still surrounding one guy's junk.

"I'm out of here."

"Not touching none of them."

We'd had enough. We had our paper and digital documentation and everyone agreed that was sufficient. It took a few hours after we got back, but that's when the jokes started. None of us had seen anything quite like that before. Every now and then the drones would catch those lone sex acts, a few instances of bestiality, but never anything like what that group was doing. What was hardest to figure out was why the whole thing hadn't broken up when they first realized we were approaching.

Eventually I came to the conclusion that I shouldn't question too much the why of people's behavior, particularly there and particularly under those circumstances.

We went out a few more times, but the operations were uneventful. I spent a lot of my last hours just cleaning up so that the new element coming in would have things neat and clean. That was maybe the only thing about the deployment for which I can use those words.

For the first time out of all my deployments, I arrived back at Fort Benning in time to go to Walmart when other shoppers were going to be in the store. Jessica was there to meet me, and after a long, long embrace we walked toward our car. A bunch of the guys wanted me to join them out at the bars, but I passed on that. I'd done it once; alcohol and being freshly back home is not a good mix. The transition is always going to be tough, and having people wanting to fight you or confront you about things when you're still in a kill-or-be-killed state can get you in a lot of trouble.

Just before we got to the car, our CQ, our company quartermaster, a really good guy named Lyons, came up to me.

"Just wanted to make sure you have everything squared away," he said, shaking my hand.

"Yeah. Thanks for your help with all the gear and stuff."

"No problem, Irv."

Behind him, I could see another Ranger standing there. He was an E4 and I could see that he was a cherry guy, freshly shaved, quiet, standing there at parade rest.

Lyons introduced us. "Sergeant," he said, "I wanted to meet you. All due respect but I heard you killed a bunch of guys. You set some record. I want to break it. I want my deployment to be just like yours was."

I couldn't believe what he was saying. Nobody says that. Nobody says that in front of a man's wife.

Jessica stood there staring at me, looking like she was trying to figure something out, remember a phone number or something that someone had asked her for, something from her past she wanted to bring back up.

I looked at the cherry new guy, held his gaze until he backed his eyes off me, and said, very quietly but very firmly, "No. You don't."

At the store we got some beer and I picked up the latest version of Madden football for my Xbox. I was twenty-three years old. I'd killed thirty-three men in less than four months. I didn't care if that first night back I was enjoying myself like a thirteen-year-old might have. Thirteen's a lucky age to be. So was twenty-three. The biggest difference between them was that at twenty-three you counted your blessings, knew that your luck could run out at any time, and didn't do too much to press it, figuring that ninety-three was a good age to be as well.

Afterword

That first night, I'd been asleep for an hour when Jessica jumped out of bed. I immediately thought someone had broken into the house, so I grabbed my gun. Ever since my first deployment when we were required to sleep with a weapon nearby, I'd kept my pistol on the nightstand or under my pillow.

"What is it?"

Jessica stood there crying quietly, her shoulders quaking, her fists bunched up beneath her eyes.

"I felt you jumping, twitching." She sat down on a blanket chest across from me. "I thought you were scared. That it was PTSD or something."

I got up and sat next to her and put my arm around her. I'd left the gun on the nightstand. "I don't remember dreaming anything. I'm okay."

We spent the rest of the night talking about a lot of the things you've just read. In some ways, I wish that new sniper had kept his damn mouth shut, but in other ways he gave me a reason to open mine up. For the first time, I made a real effort to explain to Jessica what it was like for me and how I felt I had to handle things. She asked the hard questions. How do you do it? Do you miss being over there? Do you miss killing people? She's not a sniper, but she's got good focus and aim.

I don't know if anybody who hasn't done what we've done can understand this, but in my mind, there's a me and there's a him. *He* did those things when deployed, and it's therefore easier for *me* to not think about it or talk about it. That doesn't mean that once you flip that switch or whatever, everything is okay. Everybody is going to handle things differently. I'm glad that one of the only real bad effects I felt immediately was that I became an almost-shoplifter. After that long night of talking with Jessica, I went out the next morning to get a Gatorade. I went back to the Walmart, picked up a couple of bottles, and walked out the door. The siren went off and then it hit me. I have to pay for this stuff. Over there, you just grabbed what you wanted and took it back to your room. It didn't work like that here.

I apologized and explained and paid. Good thing the people around the base understood. Other little things bothered me. I wanted to come back home and have things be exactly as they were before. Just pick up where I'd left off, as if it was going to go like this: Good-bye, honey. Kiss. Work. Hello, honey, I'm home. How was your day? Nothing in between.

Reality is different. I got home and the bed was now up against a different wall. The TV was not in the same spot. I was about to lose it and start screaming, but I had to check myself. That kind of aggression, as if someone in the platoon had messed with my weapon and not put things back where they were, would be okay over there. Not here. Things can't be exactly as I left them or as I want them to be.

He's not welcome in this house, but *you* are.

It didn't take me long to realize that I no longer wanted to be welcome in the army. Going out intact and on top was as good a way as any to end things. Still, the competitive fires were smoldering. I got a call from sniper section and was asked to represent the Rangers in the International Sniper Competition. I was honored to do it. I finished fourth out of sixty-three and had a great time. That got me thinking that this army life wasn't so bad. I should just re-up for four more. Jessica said that I should do whatever made me happy and she'd support me.

I thought more about it. I thought back to that kid who had told his recruiter to sign him up for thirty years. He was naïve, obviously, and really gung ho. That's a potent combination. I had no real frame of reference. What did thirty years really mean when you've only been on the planet for seventeen? That concept just doesn't even fit in your still developing brain.

Ultimately, despite all the things the army was willing to do to keep me around, I left. March 10, 2010, was a very fun and very scary day. I didn't have anything planned for my future. For so long, all I knew and thought about was a career in the military. As a sniper, I was used to planning and executing and taking in intel and making choices. I didn't want to be subject to a rigid schedule anymore. I needed some time and space to figure out what was going to come next. Right then, I was tired of looking through a scope and targeting things. I wanted to take in the bigger picture—find out who else and what else I could be on my own.